Manual for Innovative SMEs by Gender and Age in the Baltic Sea Region

By Alexander Frevel and Kathrin Fügel

Published and edited by
Baltic Sea Academy e.V.
Dr Max Hogefoster
Blankeneser Landstrasse 7,
22587 Hamburg, Germany

Editorial Correspondence: editor@baltic-sea-academy.eu

Printed by:
BoD-Books on Demand, Norderstedt, Germany

ISBN 9783735791405

Part-financed by the European Union (European Development Fund and European Neighbourhood and Partnership Instrument) within the QUICK IGA project. This publication does not necessarily reflect the opinion of the European Commission.

We are very grateful to the European Commission for the financial support and also to the Joint Technical Secretariat of the INTERREG IVB Programme for the support and advice.

Content

Foreword

The project "Innovative SMEs by Gender and Age (QUICK-IGA)" addresses the following objectives:

- levelling of equal opportunities for women south of the Baltic Sea with the ones of northern countries;
- strengthening the promotion of innovation in small and medium-sized enterprises by developing working cultures that explicitly improve the equal opportunities of women;
- supporting regional development in order to optimally develop human capital and competitiveness through gender and education policy.

On four levels the project focuses on the following activities:

1. Individuals: boosting motivation and work ability, thus increasing the rate of women participating in working life, through the training and education of consultants and the development of a manual;

2. Enterprises: fostering working conditions that meet women's needs and personnel development through the transfer of best practice, qualifications and coaching.

3. Organisations: competences and commitment of 45 chambers and 15 universities to supporting innovation and equal opportunities.

4. Policy: developing a strategy programme, five regional/national agreements and two action programmes to promote equal opportunities and innovation in SMEs.

The outputs and results of the project were published in the Baltic Sea Academy series for the following activities:

Data and principles

Two investigations were carried out for the countries and regions of the Baltic Sea region as the consistent basis for all further work:

a)   demographic and economic analysis in the BSR countries and regions;

b)   analysis of regional education and labour markets.

The results of these investigations were published in spring 2013 as part of the Baltic Sea Academy series under the title "Economic Perspectives, Qualification and Labour Market Integration of Women in the Baltic Sea Region".

Education

The results of the analysis have been incorporated into two new education products:

a) concept and curriculum for a train the trainer programme for the permanent implementation of training courses for consultants by universities and academies;

b) concept and curricula for a training and coaching programme for consultants to enhance their advisory competences on improving work structures in SMEs in order to increase the labour participation of women and older people, as well as innovation capacities.

Both training courses have been trialled multiple times in various locations and scientifically evaluated. The curricula, lecturer slides, execution instructions and evaluation results have been published in the form of a handbook.

Best practice

Analysis and preparation of 10 best practice cases on the promotion of labour market participation by women and older people, especially from Denmark, Sweden, Norway and Finland and transfer to the countries south of the Baltic Sea. The specific national conditions were investigated in order to allow implementation in the recipient countries.

The analysis of the conditions for the transfer of best practices and the 10 best practices have been published in the Baltic Sea Academy series of publications.

Regional/national cooperation's

Drafting and completion of memoranda of understanding on promoting innovative SMEs through women's entrepreneurship, and the increased employment of women and older people in Latvia, Lithuania, Belarus, North Poland and North Germany.

The memoranda containing the support activities to be implemented by the signatory institutions have been published in a manual.

Strategy programme

Strategic programme to promote innovation and the labour market participation of women and older people in SMEs as well as to increase the attractiveness of regional labour markets.

The strategy programme and two action plans (see below) were published as part of the Baltic Sea Academy series of publications.

Action plans

In order to involve 50 economic chambers and 16 universities in all the Baltic Sea countries in promoting the employment of women and older people in SMEs on a permanent basis, two action programmes have been developed and enacted:

a) action programme for 50 SME promoters (chambers + associations) in all BSR countries on promoting higher labour market participation by women and older people and, thus, increasing innovation capacities in SMEs;

b) action programme for 16 academies/universities from 9 Baltic Sea countries on the promotion and qualification of consultants to support the labour market participation of women and older people.

The action plans and appendix were published alongside the strategy programme (see above) in the Baltic Sea Academy series of publications.

International consultancy and transfer conferences

In order to achieve the highest possible and sustainable implementation of the target project results across all the Baltic Sea Countries, in 2013 and 2014 written transfer was supported by two consultancy and transfer conferences lasting several days with representatives from all the Baltic Sea countries. All the presentations and consultancy results developed were published in the Baltic Sea Academy series of publications in the following articles:

a) Corporate Social Responsibility and Women`s Entrepreneurship around the Mare Balticum.

b) Innovative SMEs by Gender and Age around the Mare Balticum.

Country-specific activities

During the project, it became clear that there was a need for more in-depth, further-reaching work in some countries to the south of the Baltic Sea. The following additional activities were also carried out to cover this:

Germany

Analysis of businesswomen in Germany, including a survey.

Poland

a) organisation and evaluation of a conference on "Development of the competitiveness of enterprises in the context of demographic challenges";

b) analysis and elaboration on the employment of women and older people and its promotion;

c) analysis of women's activities in SMEs in Poland and scenarios for possible future development.

Lithuania

Theoretical analytical study of political activities: Building the socially responsible employment policy in Baltic states

The results of these five additional activities were published in the Baltic Sea Academy series of publications.

Manual

Development and publication of a manual on promoting innovation through increasing the labour market participation of women and older people and the proportion of female entrepreneurs in SMEs.

The book incorporates the manual containing all the project results and additional tools for the management of demographic change at enterprise level.

The aim of the current manual is to increase innovation capacities through higher labour participation of women and elders in SMEs. It focuses on boosting motivation and workability, thus increasing the rate of women an elderly participating in work life. The results of the economic and labour market analyses and the BSR-wide study of Best Practice support measures (see WP 3) as well as the results and experiences of the Train the Trainer programme, the training and coaching programme for consultants and existing instruments for the management of demographic change at the enterprise will be evaluated systematically and combined in the manual. Beyond that the manual will contain a literature review, experiences of the project partners, information and contact details of advisory offices and supporting institutions etc.

The main target groups of the manual are

- women, elders, and owners or managers of SMEs as well as

- consultants, getting motivated by Best practice approaches to perform their tasks

Each Best practice contains a reference to the contact person.

The manual has been developed in 2013 as part of the project QUICK-IGA by Schwerin Chamber of Skilled Crafts (general management), Hanseatic-Parliament (revision and translation), Hamburg Institute of International Economics (section 2.), Vilnius Chamber of Commerce, Industry and Crafts, The Latvian Chamber of Commerce and Industry, The Chamber of Craftsmanship and Enterprise in Białystok (section 3.), Gdansk University of Technology (section 4.), Satakunta University of Applied Sciences, Vilnius University (section 5.), Work and Future (section 6. and 7.).

1. Introduction

Lack of qualified staff is one of the main reasons for SMEs to not being as innovative as possible. At the same time the available human resources (HR) are not fully employed. In the Baltic Sea Region (BSR) the labour participation of women and elders is very low particularly in the countries south of the Baltic Sea. The employment rate of women ranges from 53 % in Poland to 74 % in Norway, the rate of older people from 32 % in Poland to 70 % in Sweden. Working and organizational forms that enhance innovation capacities encourage the employment of women and elders vice versa.

This project supports the development of working and organizational structures in SMEs in order to increase the employment rate of women and elderly and concurrently increases innovation capacities (Priority 1.1). Concrete solutions for a strong BSR to be developed: increasing the innovation potential through adjusted working and organizational structures and increased number of employed elderly and women, decreasing regional disparities, improving innovation absorption capacities also in rural areas through specific solutions for each spatial type (e.g. rural areas, areas with development centres, agglomerations etc.), responses to demographic challenges, supporting innovation of SMEs.

The following objectives will be pursued:

- Levelling of equal opportunities for women south of the Baltic Sea with the ones of northern countries
- Strengthening the promotion of innovation in small and medium enterprises by developing working cultures, which explicitly improve the equal opportunities of women
- Supporting the regional development in order to optimally develop the human capital and competitiveness through gender and education policy.

The project partnership has been established to reflect both the geographic and functional diversity of the project objectives:

- Hanseatic Parliament, Germany
- Schwerin Chamber of Skilled Crafts, Germany

- Hamburg Institute of International Economics, Germany
- Work and Future, Germany
- Gdansk University of Technology, Poland
- Bialystok Foundation of Professional Training, Poland
- Lithuanian University of Educational Sciences, Lithuania
- State Education Centre, Latvia
- Minsk Department of the Belarusian Chamber of Commerce and Industry
- Brest Department of Belarusian Chamber of Commerce and Industry
- Satakunta University of Applied Sciences, Finland
- Norden Association, Sweden
- The Nordic Forum of Crafts, Norway

The Baltic Sea Region (BSR) is challenged by demographic change like nearly all European regions and countries. The starting point shows a similar situation, but at second glance there are big differences among the countries.

The current situation shows a polarisation between the Northwest and the Southeast. Denmark, Finland, Germany, Norway, Sweden and the United Kingdom often have more positive values than the EU-average, whereas the indicators for Estonia, Latvia, Lithuania and Poland are below average. An important exception is the fertility rate in Germany which has been and remains the lowest behind Poland.

The expected development (in this comparison we used data up to 2050) shows a growing disparity between the countries. Due to low birth rates the proportion of the younger population will decline mainly in Germany, Latvia, Lithuania and Poland. At the same time the working age population will decrease (most in Estonia, Germany, Latvia, Lithuania and Poland; least in the United Kingdom) and the share of the elderly will grow (most in Germany and Poland; least in Denmark, Norway, Sweden and UK).

Demographic change is irreversible in the short and medium term. The only way to maintain or raise the given amount of population could be significant increases of birth rates. All other possibilities necessarily mean a) to exploit the labour market reserve by increasing the employment rate of the elderly, the younger, the unemployed and the women (internal solution) or b) to integrate a more or less high number of immigrated people.

2. Economic Perspectives, Qualification and Labour Market Integration of Women in the Baltic Sea Region – Abstract

2.1 Introduction

Demographic and economic structural change will affect the development of the whole Baltic Sea Region in the future. Coping with these challenges requires initiatives aiming at labour market issues. A shrinking and ageing labour force entails the danger of shortage of labour supply in general while demand for skilled labour increases in the course of knowledge-based structural change. A viable means of strengthening competitiveness and economic growth in this area is the full exploitation of its human resources. Among these an advanced integration of women in the labour market is at the top of the agenda.

In a recent comprehensive study (Biermann et al. 2013)[1], current economic and demographic structures in the Baltic Sea Region have been analysed. Additionally, development perspectives have been assessed. These overall macroeconomic conditions constitute the framework for enhancing the labour market integration of women. The abstract at hand refers to the main findings of this study.

The *outline of this abstract is as follows*: In the following section 2, current economic trends and perspectives in the Baltic Sea Region are discussed. First, the main findings are presented. Subsequently, some selected results in this context are presented. Section 3 addresses the education and labour market involvement of women in Baltic Sea Region countries. Also in this context, after having portrayed the main findings some selected results are reviewed in more detail. Section 4 concludes.

---

[1] This abstract refers to the following publication: Biermann, U.; Boll, C.; Reich, N.; Stiller, S. (2013): Economic Perspectives, Qualifications and Labour Market Integration of Women in the Baltic Sea Region, M. Hogeforster (ed.): Baltic Sea Academy 9, Norderstedt, Germany.

2.2 Regional Development in the Baltic Sea Region: Current Economic Trends and Perspectives

a) Main findings

Within the past decades, intensive integration processes between member states of the European Union (EU) could be witnessed. But also on the regional level, outstanding integration results were denoted. These kinds of processes occur as effects of spatial proximity between regions and experienced intensification in the course of fading relevance of national borders. Examples can be found around the shores of the Northern Sea or in the Alpine region connecting several European countries by a shared mountain chain.

The regional integration phenomenon in the focal point of the following survey is the Baltic Sea Region. Despite being aware of that within Interreg IV B, in the following it is marked as a broader geographic region.

It comprises the Mare Balticum with its bordering countries Denmark, Estonia, Finland, Latvia, Lithuania, Sweden as well as regions of Germany (Schleswig-Holstein, Mecklenburg-Vorpommern and Hamburg), Poland (zachodnio pomorskie, pomorskie, warmińsko-mazurskie, podlaskie) and Russia (Kaliningradskaya oblast, Leningradskaya oblast, St. Petersburg). Additionally non EU member Norway is considered in most of the analysis due to being an important trading and integration partner in the area.

With the exception of Russia, all bordering countries are members of the EU. In these countries, we find 147 million inhabitants which account for 29.3 % of total EU population. These countries are responsible for 30.3 % of corresponding gross domestic product. Looking exclusively at the Baltic Sea Region (i.e. only including those regions of Germany and Poland bordering the Baltic Sea), its EU regions produce about 8.4 % (cf. Eurostat 2012, data reference 2009) of gross domestic product of the 27 EU member states and account for a corresponding population of 8.0 % (cf. Eurostat 2012). These figures specify the Baltic Sea Region as a significant social and economic habitat with extensive integration potentials along its national borders.

Of notable relevance for its future development prospects is the instance that the Baltic Sea Region is marked by substantial structural and developmental differences between its countries and regions. Despite various similarities, there are significant cultural, political and economic differences both between and within member states. On the one hand, we find post-transformation countries like the Baltic States which are still experiencing catching-up processes. On the other hand, we have a number of Europe's strongest economies and leading innovation regions in the north-western part of the Baltic Sea Region.

Additionally important for the future development of the Baltic Sea Region is the founded prognosis that several factors influencing its socioeconomic development will experience considerable changes during the upcoming years. The framework of its socioeconomic development will change due to continuing integration and convergence processes, the structural change towards a service and knowledge-based economy, intensified trade, labour market networking and an overall demographic change. These factors bring about a number of challenges but may also be used as unique opportunities for developing the Baltic Sea Region.

The development in Baltic States and Poland in the last decade is shaped by a strong catching-up process in terms of GDP. This development contributed extensively to on-going convergence processes in core economic indicators between old and new EU members. Nevertheless, Baltic States and Poland still face far lower levels of income per capita than older EU members in the western part of the Baltic Sea region.

According to GDP forecasts until 2020, the catching-up in Baltic States and Poland will continue, even though also in the second decade of the century, considerable income per capita differences between the Eastern and the Western countries around the Baltic Sea will persist. Corresponding to GDP growth, Baltic States and Poland display promising trade perspectives.

The rapid economic growth goes hand in hand with a vast increase of labour productivity, promoted by technological progress. The overwhelming development of the service sector in the last decade and the high shares of tertiary activities and other knowledge-based branches of business in the Baltic States and Poland give rise to promising rates for these countries.

However, opposite to the vital amelioration of economic prosperity, the labour force development in this region is a cause for concern as it threatens promising employment growth. In the last decade, driven by persisting low birth rates and aggravated by disadvantageous migration balances, Baltic States denoted a halt or even shrinkage of the labour force. Poland experienced a considerable increase of the employable population.

Nevertheless until 2030, Poland will experience a faster ageing and shrinking, compared to EU-27 average. The same applies to Lithuania, Finland and Germany, whereas in Latvia and Estonia shrinking will continue on a high level but ageing will slow down. All in all, until 2020 population will decrease in all Baltic States and will persevere in Poland. Forecasts are even more drastic with respect to employable population. Beyond the labour force this collaterally affects social security systems, financial markets, and infrastructure.

In order to sustain competitiveness, but also in the context of demographic change, innovation is a central issue for all European countries. Within the knowledge-based structural change, it is the prime element enhancing further economic growth, competitiveness and wealth. These factors widely cohere with the educational level of the population, especially with the qualification of staff in the research and development sector.

Up to date, the highest shares of inhabitants with a degree in the upper and post-secondary sector can be found in Poland and the Baltic States, and within those in Lithuania. Over the last eight years, with the exception of Denmark, the share of primary and secondary educational degrees has diminished in all observed countries. The high shares of well-educated people in the Baltic Sea region, especially of the Nordic and Baltic States, are in accordance with a dominant, above European Union-average lying, tertiary sector in all the observed national economies and display a great potential in the field of innovation. But when it comes to the share of employed persons in knowledge intensive industries, these are – in contrast to the educational level of the employable population – among the lowest in the Baltic States. It can be reasoned that the potential of a highly educated population has not yet been fully utilised in all countries of the Baltic Sea region.

This should be seen as a call for action from political and economic decision makers, as these sectors are highly crucial within the structural change, especially for the generating and adaption of innovation. Here, spatial proximity will play an important role and Poland, Russia and the Baltic States will benefit from exchange and cluster effects with already knowledge-based economies such as Sweden and Finland. Hence, the reduction of border obstacles and the promotion of mobility between these countries are supported by another just cause. Cross-border clustering plays a major role within knowledge-based growth. It largely depends on spatial proximity and face-to-face contacts, which promote exchange between businesses and the development of networks and cluster effects. Good examples for cross-border clusters in the Baltic Sea region are the health sector and the creative industry. As great innovation potentials, environmental technology and energy supply can also be named.

However, additional challenges for future development of the Baltic Sea region arise from distinct socioeconomic disparities on the regional level. Regional population development can to a great extent be ascribed to extensive urbanisation processes: As economic centres, cities attract international migrants as well as the local population. Their central role within the economy and as a location for work and life can further be explained by their pioneering role within knowledge intensive industries. Thus, the importance of cities as driving forces of regional growth will further increase. Despite prevalent structural differences between eastern and western member states and on-going convergence processes on country levels, the big cities will keep their outstanding role as triggers of structural change.

Demographic change and the afore-mentioned challenges of fostering catching-up processes, innovation power and value added requires, alongside with the promotion of immigration, an efficient use of domestic human resources. This task comprises on the one hand a sufficient and market-adequate formation of human capital via the educational system and on the other hand a high labour market involvement of those resources. A special focus has to be given to the exploitation of women's potentials in this context.

b) Selected results on socio-economic conditions

Highly relevant for the future economic development perspectives of the Baltic Sea Region are its **demographic conditions**. Among other influencing factors, demography has impacts on labour supply, demand for infrastructure and public finances.

The Baltic Sea Region faces a number of demographic challenges, among which the demographic change of its populations due to declining birth rates and growing life expectancies, as well as increasing urbanisation can be found. It could be observed that while ageing is a global trend, shrinking populations are a rather local phenomenon (Kühntopf and Tivig 2009). Population development generally results from natural population development, namely births and deceases, and from migration movements. Table 1 gives an overview of the named indicators.

Table 1 Demographic Indicators

	Fertility rate	Expectancy of life at birth in years				net migration
	2010[1]	2000[2]	2010[3]	2010	2010[1]	2000[2]
		Men	Women	Men	Women	
Denmark	1.87	74.5	79.2	77.2	81.4	16,847
Germany	1.39	75.1	81.2	78.0	83.0	130,166
Estonia	1.63	65.2	76.2	70.6	80.8	32
Finland	1.87	74.2	81.2	76.9	83.5	13,756
Latvia	1.17	64.7	76.0	68.6	78.4	-7,912
Lithuania	1.55	66.8	77.5	68.0	78.9	-77,944
Norway	1.95	76	81.5	79	83.3	42,163
Poland	1.38	69.9	78.0	72.1	80.7	-2,114
Russia	1.54	59.0	72.3	62.8	74.7	49,734
Sweden	1.98	77.4	82.0	79.6	83.6	1,181,595

[1] for Russia data from 2009
[2] for Latvia and EU27 data from 2002
[3] for Russia and EU27 data from 2009

Sources: Eurostat (2012/2013); Federal Statistical Office Russia (2011); HWWI.

While the preservation **fertility rate** lies at 2.1 children per woman, only Sweden, Denmark and Finland approach a rate of two children per woman. The lowest fertility rates can be found in Poland, Germany and Latvia. Within these countries, low fertility rates have been persistent during the past decades. For the upcoming years, population forecasts by Eurostat are based on the assumption that fertility behaviour is not going to change substantially. Therefore, natural population development is expected to have negative impacts in the Baltic Sea Region.

In the course of the past decade, **life expectancy** has risen in all countries with Sweden exhibiting the highest expectancy for both sexes (men 79.6 years/ women 83.6 years). Nevertheless, life expectancy in the Baltic States, Poland and Russia is still clearly lower than in the EU on average. For the future, increasing life expectancy is anticipated for these countries due to several factors, e.g. increasing per capita income, better nutrition and improved environmental conditions.

A highly critical factor for the overall population development is **net migration**. It can be decisive for whether countries are growing or shrinking. Most countries in the Baltic Sea Region attract more people from abroad than exhibiting causes to emigrate. Yet, net migration is negative in Latvia, Lithuania and in relation to population only slightly negative in Poland, where more people emigrated than immigrated in 2010. However, since the 1990s a large amount of people emigrated from these countries to western EU countries. A positive migration balance, preferably with skilled workers immigrating, could meet the challenges arising for the labour force in the course of the demographic change. However, migration patterns aggravate natural population development in most cases. The negative migration balances are therefore to be seen as highly critical for the labour market, which in turn is a critical determinant within the structural change towards knowledge-based economies. Reasons for strong emigrations are among others the considerable wage differentials between the eastern and western countries (Brücker et al 2009).

As regards changes of the employable population, forecasts are particularly drastic in the Baltic States, Poland and Russia. This corresponds with the change of population by age groups depicted in figure 1. Here, it can be noted that in the named countries, the decline in population aged 15 to 44 will be most severe. The same holds for Germany. As this is the younger fraction of the employable population, outlooks for the time past 2030 are similarly negative.

Figure 1

Change of Population by Age Group 2010 to 2030

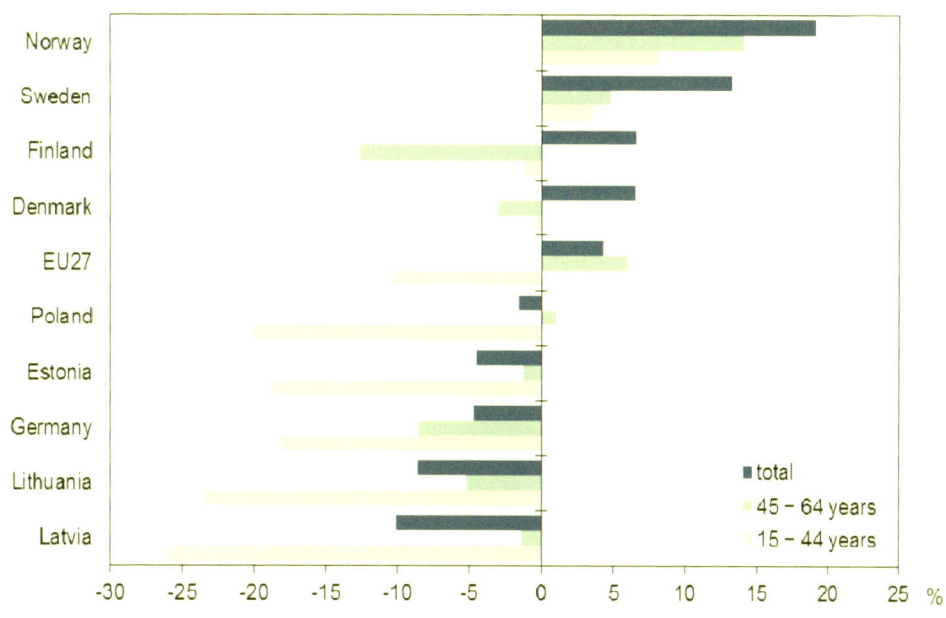

Sources Eurostat (2012) Eurostat (2013) HWWI

Demographic changes influence the economic development of the Baltic Sea Region. Social security systems, financial markets, infrastructure and labour force are collaterally affected. Due to varying initial positions, the demographic change and its effects on production preconditions and development potentials - especially on the labour market - will assume different shapes within the regions around the Baltic Sea (Stiller and Wedemeier 2011 b). For many countries, central tasks are to preserve the employable population as long as possible as a part of the active population and to address migration as a threat for labour force development.

In order to sustain competitiveness with other countries, but also in the context of demographic change, innovation is a central issue for all European countries. Within the knowledge-based structural change, it is the prime element enhancing further economic growth and value adding (Bundesministerium für Bildung und Forschung

2007). For the higher income countries in the Baltic Sea Region, innovation is a tool to stay assertive on global markets. For those countries still going through a process of catching-up, innovation is a measure to accelerate these processes. However, there are differing regional conditions for profiting from innovation.

Looking at the development of gross domestic product, a rapid process of convergence on the national level could be viewed. Yet, observations on the regional level exhibit heterogeneous dynamics as illustrated in the following map (see figure 2). Similar to the national level, a clear gap between eastern and north-western regions around the Baltic Sea can be determined. Whereas western German, Danish, Swedish and most Finish regions exhibited increases of less than 50 %, almost all regions in Poland and the Baltic States denoted rates of 50 up to 120 % growth.

Figure 2

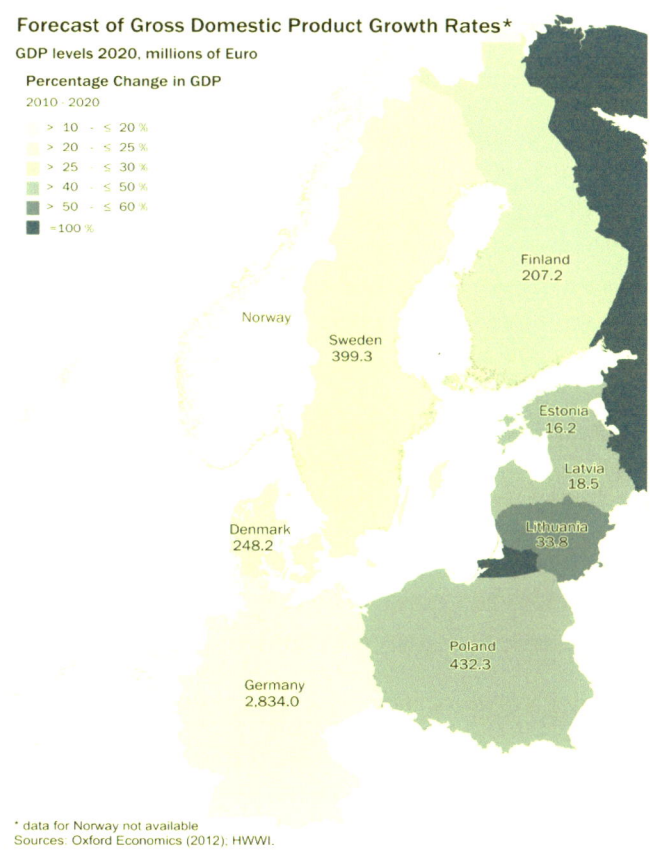

Forecast of Gross Domestic Product Growth Rates*

GDP levels 2020, millions of Euro

Percentage Change in GDP
2010 - 2020

- > 10 - ≤ 20 %
- > 20 - ≤ 25 %
- > 25 - ≤ 30 %
- > 40 - ≤ 50 %
- > 50 - ≤ 60 %
- > 100 %

Finland
207.2

Norway

Sweden
399.3

Estonia
16.2

Latvia
18.5

Denmark
248.2

Lithuania
33.8

Poland
432.3

Germany
2,834.0

* data for Norway not available
Sources: Oxford Economics (2012); HWWI.

Generally, regional growth perspectives depend on several factors, e.g. demographics, economic structure, educational level, innovative potential and the macroeconomic environment. The analyses clearly show strong regional disparities regarding economic and demographic structures as well as dynamics. Altogether, regions in the Baltic Sea Region exhibit heterogeneous conditions for future development.

2.3 Women in Baltic Sea Region countries – education and labour market involvement

a) Main findings

Demographic change and the aforementioned challenges of fostering catching-up processes, innovation power and value added requires, alongside with promoting migration, an efficient use of domestic human resources. This task comprises a sufficient and market-adequate formation of human capital via the educational system and a high labour market involvement of those resources. Thereby a high priority has to be given to a better utilisation of the skills and experience of women. This section solely refers to data at national level provided by Eurostat.

The population of the Baltic Sea area comprises employed, unemployed and economically inactive people as the three main categories. To a more or less extent, all three categories address the problem of untapped resources.

Firstly, this is the case referring to employed[2] persons who aim at working more hours (underemployed part-timers); furthermore, working life duration and earned income point to some extent to underused potentials. Unemployed persons, although signalling a strong labour market affiliation, fail to realise a satisfactory job match and therefore represent a reasonable share of the labour force that is actually not in productive use. Last but not least, a reasonable part of economically inactive people is closely attached to the labour market and thus has to be regarded as potentially additional labour force. Inactive persons are those who are neither classified as employed nor as unemployed. The economically inactive make up more than one third of the EU-27 population in working age. Among them, 11 million persons are rather close to the labour market and therefore have to be regarded as a potentially additional labour force.

---

[2] According to Eurostat, employed persons are persons who are aged 15 year and over (16 and over in ES, UK and SE (1995-2001); 15-74 years in DK, EE, HU, LV, FI and SE (from 2001 onwards); 16-74 in IS and NO), who during the reference week performed work, even for just one hour a week, for pay, profit or family gain, or who were not at work but had a job or business from which they were temporarily absent because of, e.g., illness, holidays, industrial dispute or education and training.

The analysis of human resources in terms of education, labour market involvement and job features yields a quite sophisticated performance of Baltic Sea region countries. While some findings that refer to gender differences display great similarities between countries, the cross-country comparison is shaped by clearly pronounced national characteristics in other aspects which shall be resumed in what follows.

For the Baltic States, it is observed that the share of women graduating from university is far higher than men's and that, in a cross-country perspective, highly educated women are very well integrated into the labour market. Nevertheless, the overall employment rate of women is quite low in Baltic States and lowest in Poland, being negatively connected to the number of children whereas the positive association to the youngest child's age is less pronounced in this region. Part-time as well as temporary employment is scarce and moreover, many women experience to be involuntary part-timers. As to the gender patterns of work remuneration, Baltic States shape a heterogeneous pattern: Whereas Lithuania and Latvia (together with Poland) display quite gender balanced gross hourly incomes, the Estonian gender pay gap is outstanding and highest among all countries observed. This is striking in light of the comparatively high share of women among managers, technicians and (associate) professionals. Another common feature of the Baltic States is the lower unemployment rate of women compared to men. But once without a job, women face, like their male counterparts, a high risk of persistent unemployment. Furthermore, there is a reasonable share of potentially additional labour force among the inactive population in Latvia and Estonia. To a considerable extent, this may be attributed to job search frustration: In Latvia, almost every seventh (Estonia: every twelfth) inactive women does not expect to find a job. Moreover and for both sexes, there is a great potential to enhance income perspectives over the life course via a stronger engagement in life-long learning. Among all countries observed, Baltic States and Poland come last in this aspect.

In Poland, traditional gender roles are very common. Polish women experience the lowest employment rate in a cross-country comparison and the highest gender gap in employment, which even increased over the last decade. On the one hand, the poor pre-school childcare provision does not seem to hinder mothers' employment, but, on the other hand, despite a quite well established child care provision for children aged six to eleven, Poland displays the lowest employment rate of mothers of children in this age group. In contrast to the Baltic States, temporary employment is very widespread for both sexes and applies mostly to full-time work, whereas part-time employment is as rare as in the Baltic neighbour countries. Poland exhibits the highest share of inactive persons among females among all countries observed: One third of the female population aged 25 to 64 is inactive, and the share even increased over the last decade. Retirement is the dominant motivation for being inactive among women in this age group. Maybe due to the poor provision of flexible working time arrangements that result in more unisex work patterns of the employed, Poland exhibits the lowest unadjusted gender pay gap among all countries observed.

The Scandinavian countries seem to have overcome gender differences in the labour market to a great extent. The overall high labour market integration of mothers is related to a vast provision of childcare for children below three and a high extent of full-day care provision. However, the connection between mothers' employment and children's age is much more pronounced in Finland than in Scandinavian neighbour countries. Conversely, Denmark ranks highest as neither children's age nor their number is reasonably associated to mothers' employment. Nevertheless, the share of women in the three highest occupational statuses is comparatively low in Denmark, as well as in Norway (and Germany). Another finding is that Swedish (and German) women are mostly harmed by precarious work forms. Furthermore, Scandinavian countries face higher unadjusted gender wage gaps than Latvia, Lithuania and Poland. Another striking finding in this context is that in Scandinavian countries, education does not pay off very well to reduce the gender pay gap: Women's relative income in terms of men's worsens with the educational level attained. This holds, in contrast to Poland and Germany, also for medium level of education. The relationship is most pronounced in Finland. With respect to the productive use of female skills, Denmark and Sweden perform best.

Germany is the second country with rather strong traditional gender roles in its western part. One outcome on the national level is the low childcare provision for children aged zero to three. In this context, the particularly low employment rate of mothers with children below three does not come at surprise, neither the strong difference in employment rates between childless women and mothers. Tertiary education does not pay off in terms of gendered labour market prospects: Only in

Germany women holding a university degree experience a lower employment rate than men, and their relative income in terms of men's worsens if they attain a university degree. If women work at all, they do this mostly in part-time forms: Germany displays the highest part-time ratio of employed women among all countries observed. Thus, the low share of women among managers, technicians and (associate) professionals comes as no surprise. Motivation for part-time is driven by family context. Due to the overall high magnitude of part-time, there is a reasonable amount of underemployed part-timers as a potentially additional workforce. Furthermore, only in Germany the part-time incidence as well as the gender pay gap – ranking as the second highest level among all countries observed – increase steadily with age.

Despite these marked differences, the gendered structure of education and labour market involvement in the BSR region also features some cross-country similarities.

Women are better educated than men in most countries of the Baltic Sea region. Women leave school less often without a degree, and they are involved in tertiary education to a higher extent. In all countries but Germany, employed women are on average better educated than men. Nevertheless, a traditional gendered segregation of occupations and by field of study is observed in all countries of the Baltic Sea region. This might be one reason for the gender gap in pay for all educational groups that is also visible in all BSR countries. The employment rate of females is lower than for males in the BSR, but the gap is smaller in the youngest age group. Family duties (number and age of children) are negatively associated to women's employment rate in most countries except for Denmark and Sweden, but not to men's.

b) Selected results on education and employment

Education and training is an essential part of human capital formation. Educational systems have to be optimized to efficiently equip people with knowledge and competences that are needed in a permanently changing environment. This applies to the public educational system as well as to forms of vocational training. Moreover, in the context of continuous economic, demographic and technological change, education has evolved to become a life-long business to maintain a nation's competitiveness, welfare and employability of its workforce.

Figure 3 shows the percentage of adult population aged 25 to 64 participating in education and training. Participation is defined as having received education or training in the four weeks preceding the survey. The percentage refers to the share of participants in relation to the total population in the corresponding age group.[3] Most countries experienced growing participation rates in education and training in the last decade. For males, the sole exception is Sweden with a lower rate in 2010 compared to 2000. As to gender, women experienced a higher engagement than men in all countries, and this trend is stable over time. For both sexes, Scandinavian countries, headed by Denmark, displayed the highest participation rates. In 2010, they ranged from 16 % for Norwegian men to 39.1 % for Danish women. Estonia was in a medium position and performed better than Germany, Poland, Latvia and Lithuania.

Figure 3

Share of adult population aged 25 to 64 participating in education and training

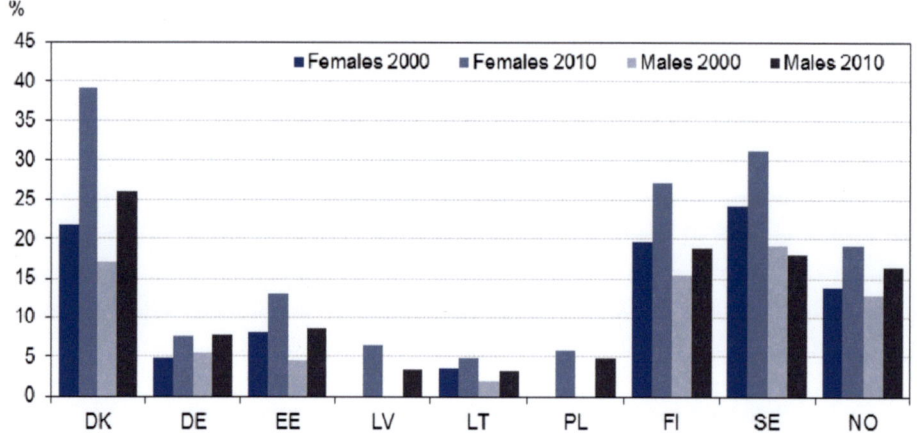

Note: No data available for LV and PL 2000.
Sources: Eurostat (2012a); HWWI.

---

[3] The data originate from the EU Labour Force Survey. The information collected relates to all education or training whether or not relevant to the respondent's current or possible future job. It includes formal and non-formal education and training that means in general activities in the school/university systems but also courses, seminars workshops, etc. outside the formal education and regardless their topic.

The **employment rate** of women with children is related to the age of their youngest child in all countries in the BSR, as seen in figure 4. Participating in the labour market seems to be particularly difficult to reconcile with family duties for mothers with young children. In most countries, women's employment increases as the youngest child becomes older. Once the child reaches school age, mothers' employment rate stays fairly the same in most countries of the Baltic Sea region. Mothers were best integrated into the labour market in Denmark, where the employment rate ranged between 81 % and 87 % in the three categories of the youngest child's age, and Sweden (78 %, 89 % and 92 %, respectively). Among mothers with children below the age of six, the employment rate was highest in Denmark, Lithuania and Sweden. The rate was low in Estonia, Poland, Finland and Germany.

Figure 4

Employment rate by age of youngest child of females aged 25 to 54 in 2011

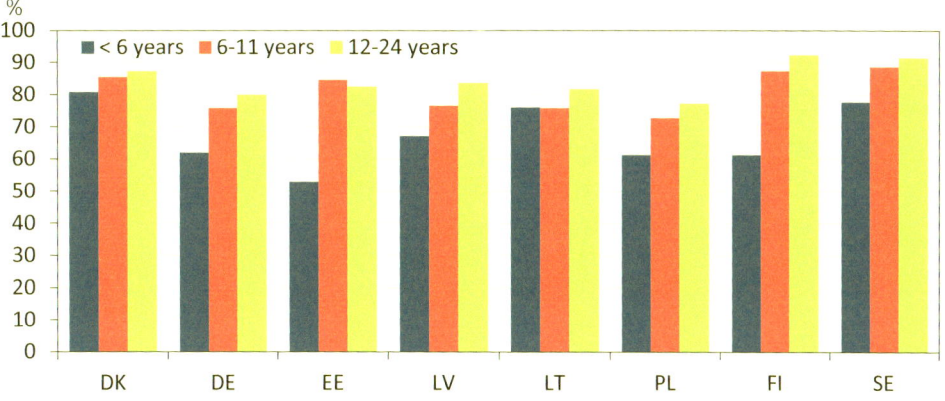

Note: child has to be in full social and economic dependence from other household member/-s (parents/ adults).
Sources: Eurostat (2012a); HWWI.

In the BSR, **women's earnings** were on average between 5 and 30 percentage points lower than men's in 2006 and 2010 (figure 5). The unadjusted gender pay gap turned out to be highest in Germany and Estonia, whereas it was lowest in Poland. This holds for 2006 as well as for 2010. The gap changed only slightly during this time span. In most countries it decreased somewhat, but the two countries which experienced a gap increase are Latvia and Germany. In other words, for women in Latvia and Germany the earnings distance to men increased during these years.

Figure 5

Gender pay gap in unadjusted form

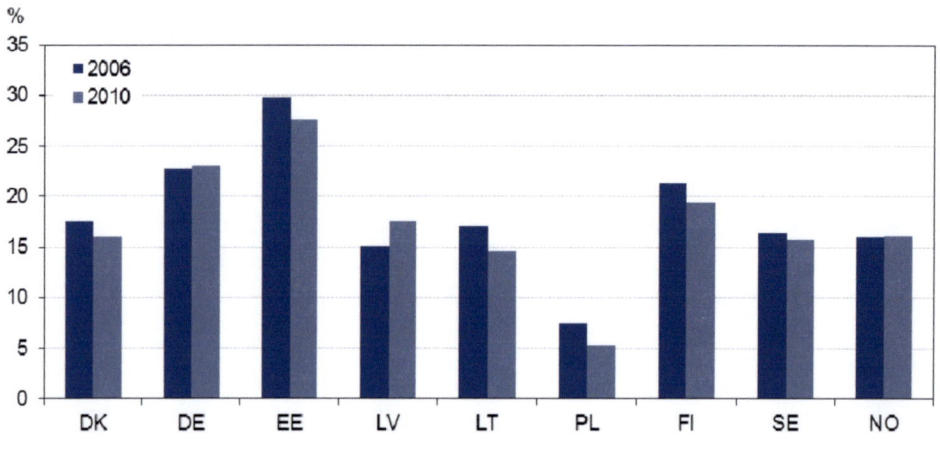

Sources: Eurostat (2012a); HWWI.

The gender pay gap reflects the gendered distribution of occupational status in the BSR countries. To a certain extent, the most pronounced gap in Estonia, Germany and Finland may be attributed to the comparatively low share of managers and/or professionals among women in these countries.

Members of the population of working age who are without a job have to be considered as untapped resources. In the context of ageing societies and an increasing demand of skilled workers the full exploitation of potentials becomes more and more important. **Unemployed persons** are those aged 15-74[4] who were without work during the reference week but currently available for work, and who were either actively seeking work in the past four weeks or who had already found a job to start within the next three months. Unemployment rates represent unemployed persons as a percentage of the active population.

---

[4] (in Sweden (1995-2000) and Norway: 16-74)

For women and men in all BSR countries, the risk of unemployment decreased with increasing educational level in 2011 (figure 6). Compared to women in the medium age group, the employment bonus of women graduating from university was particularly high in Lithuania. The same is found for men. Among women and men with a low educational level, the unemployment rate was clearly highest in the Baltic States, with Lithuania exhibiting the highest rates with 38 % among women and 40 % among men. But also Poland, Sweden and Finland were above the EU-27 average for the unemployment rate of women in this educational group (16.6 %), and the Baltic States and Poland were above the EU-27 average for men.

Figure 6

Unemployment by educational level and sex of persons aged 15 to 64 i

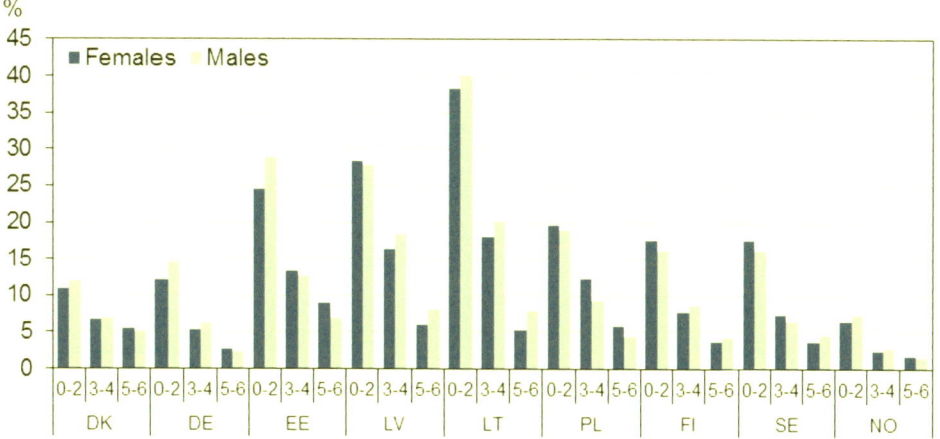

Note: 0-2: Pre-primary, primary and lower secondary education. 3-4: Upper secondary and post-secondary non-tertiary education. 5-6: First and second stage of tertiary education

Sources: Eurostat (2012a), HWWI

2.4   Conclusion

For the future of the Baltic Sea Region it can be stated that the catching-up process of its eastern states will continue. Continuing convergence processes will lead to an increased assimilation of income levels in eastern and western countries. However, due to large disparities in regional structures in the Baltic Sea region, the impacts of convergence will vary between its regions. Cities are regional and national centres of economic development. They take over a leading role within the knowledge-based structural change.

Generally, there is a high potential for knowledge-based structural change in this areas. Here, the strengthening of research and development activities in public sectors and firms is a central field of action. Additionally, cross-border integration and cluster building are effective measures for developing R&D-networks. The support of migration of labour forces and infrastructure investments in order to increase mobility are exemplary tasks.

In the course of the structural change towards knowledge-based industries, special attention should be paid to cities as engines of regional development. Crucial aspects for the development of cities are whether or not they will be able to cope and counter steer international migration. A sufficient supply of housing and a successful integration of foreign workforces are central challenges. Soft factors, such as fostering the attractiveness of cities by an increase in quality of life are additionally important when meeting challenges and opportunities of migration.

The major task for the Baltic Sea Region is to smooth potential negative consequences of the demographic change. Measures to reduce the threatening shortage in labour force, especially in the Baltic States and Poland are in high demand. The mobilisation of less frequent workforces, such as elderly people and women is a central task for political decision makers and companies. Additionally, the improvement of the educational level of these groups, migrants and the existing labour force will be of aid against demographical deductions. The cross-border recognition of educational attainments is another factor to foster cross-border labour market integration.

To obtain an integral picture of the situation of women in the Baltic Sea region, the portrayed economic and regional perspectives of those countries have to be merged with the corresponding features of qualification and employment.

In the Baltic States and Poland – and to a certain degree this applies also to Germany – women's skills accommodate an untapped potential of considerable amount. This finding particularly applies to the suboptimal labour market usage of (high level of) formal education, to the underachievement in the provision of full-time jobs and adequate institutional child care, to the representation of women in managerial positions and among self-employed as well as to a considerable pay gap and low career prospects due to poor life-long learning opportunities in the workplace.

Furthermore, a reasonable share of highly educated women is economically inactive in those countries. On the other hand, the pronounced labour market orientation and high educational aspirations of young women especially in the Baltic States are quite promising. In Germany and Poland, traditional gender roles hinder a more extensive female integration in the labour market, whereas this obstacle plays a minor role in Scandinavian and part of Baltic countries.

However, tackling gender pay gap is a challenging task in all countries observed and will not be successful unless the gendered segregation of rather high-pay male and rather low-pay female jobs will be redressed. Whereas women in high-wage shaped Scandinavian countries and Germany are handicapped by some side effects like precarious work forms, women in the eastern countries of the Baltic Sea should use the chance of – still – quite low wages to establish a job culture that grounds on reliable work arrangements with respect to job security, working-time and income for both sexes.

The framework of the socioeconomic development in Baltic States and Poland will change due to continued integration and convergence processes, the structural change towards a service and knowledge-based economy, intensified trade, labour market networking and an overall demographic change. These factors bring about a number of challenges but may also be used as unique opportunities for developing the southern Baltic Sea countries to a "Triple A Region" in terms of skills, innovation and competitiveness. In this context, human resources, and among them particularly female potentials, should be fully tapped.

For further information, see: Hamburg Institute of International Economics.

3. National memoranda of Understanding on Promoting Innovative SMEs through Women's Entrepreneurship, Increased Employment of Women and Older People

3.1 Introduction

Five national memoranda of understanding (MOU) have been completed within the project *"Innovative SMEs by Gender and Age (QUICK-IGA)"*.

The purpose of the MOU is to ensure the proper implementation of the objectives of the QUICK-IGA project in their respective countries. It also ensures that women and men equality at work as well as support of women and older people so that they can remain occupied longer will be achieved in a timely way.

Each national MOU provides an overall interagency coordination framework between all relevant stakeholder groups.

Goals of the national memoranda:

- To ensure innovations in SMEs as the first priority.
- To support women and older people so that they can remain occupied longer.
- Committed support through the ongoing dialogue with all relevant stakeholder groups.
- To promote gender- and age-management in SMEs.
- To promote education and training in general.

By signing the memoranda, all participating institutions and organisations appreciate the initiatives developed by the project "QUICK-IGA" and basically support their implementation in their country.

3.2 Short description of the National Memoranda of Understanding of Latvia, Lithuania, Poland, Belarus and Northern Germany

3.2.1 National Memorandum of Understanding of Latvia

As the signatories of the Memorandum, representatives of government and NGOs, we commit to:

1. Ensuring innovations in SMEs as the first priority. Achieving women and men equality at work will give contribution by leveraging necessary skills to promote creativity and know-how. Sustainable promotion of the employment of women and older persons should be associated with the strengthening of regional innovation, productivity and growth. All activities are focused on the strengthening the SMEs in the interest of the public, as SMEs are the backbone of the economy and society.

2. Support of women and older people so that they can remain occupied longer, start a business or become self-employed will reduce social pressure on governments and will contribute to the quality of life of individuals. With the promotion of employment and employability, workability and entrepreneurship of, women and older people in the first place the constructive steps to handling the effects of demographic change will be made and will foster innovation driven economy.

3. The signatories appreciate the initiatives developed by the project "Innovative Small and Medium Enterprises by Gender and Age" and basically support their implementation in Latvia.

4. Committed support through the ongoing dialogue with all relevant stakeholder groups to the creation of optimal conditions in the area of policy work, business, education, culture, social area, financial area aiming at increasing level of productivity and well being of society.

5. Promoting gender- and age-management in the company for purpose of maintaining and strengthening the workability and the employability primarily of

women and older people and improving productivity through wide-ranging information and advice services to SMEs.

6. Strong commitment to the comprehensive promotion of entrepreneurship in general and of companies created by women in particular, with the target to increase significantly the number of women entrepreneurs and start-ups to secure high economic stability and the opportunity to create additional jobs.

7. Education is the main key for fostering innovation, competitiveness and creation of more jobs. Therefore the signatories would like to promote education and training in general, as well as the development and approval of entrepreneurship education policy in Latvia and the effective implementation of this policy.

8. The parties of the Memorandum recommend to form a round table, "Innovation by Gender and Age," which meets at least semi-annually, evaluates the developments being made, designs other relevant policies and measures needed, promotes networking among women and recognizes itself as a permanent advisory body for all relevant stakeholder groups, especially for politics. Representatives of women and older persons are a necessary element of this ongoing round-table. By the end of the project an institution, active in the field of economic development, should be chosen to be responsible for the future organization of the round table.

9. By undersigning the Memorandum we agree to work closely together at a strategic level in areas of common interest with the view to promoting innovations via equal opportunities for women and the development of women and older persons as employees and entrepreneurs in Latvia.

10. Other institutions and organisations are invited to join this Memorandum and to take an active part in the important social, economic and political task to promote opportunities for women and older people in the SME sector in Latvia.

Signatories:
- The Ministry of Welfare
- The Ministry of Economy
- The State Employment Agency

- The Ministry of Education and Science
- State Education Centre(VISC)
- The Ministry of Agriculture
- The Ministry of Environmental Protection and Regional Development
- The Latvian Association of Local and Regional Governments
- NGO Līder
- The Latvian Chamber of Commerce and Industry
- The Latvian Chamber of Crafts
- The University of Latvia
- The Riga Technical University
- Stakeholders for women (-employment), i.e. associations, networks and similar
- Trade unions
- Labor Office

3.2.2 National memorandum of Understanding of Lithuania

As the signatories of the memorandum we: the government representatives, non-governmental organizations, industry associations, public organizations recognize the current problematic situation and challenges faced by Lithuania, by signing this memorandum we commit to:

1. Ensure innovations in SMEs as the first priority. Achieving women and men equality at work, which will give contribution by leveraging necessary skills to promote creativity and know-how. Sustainable promotion of the employment of women and older persons should be associated with the strengthening of regional innovation, productivity and growth. All activities are focused on the strengthening the SMEs in the interest of the public, as SMEs are the backbone of the economy and society.

2. Support women and older people so that they can remain occupied longer, start a business or become self-employed which will reduce social pressure on governments and will contribute to the quality of life of individuals. With the promotion of employment and employability, workability and entrepreneurship of, women and older people in the first place the constructive steps to handling

the effects of demographic change will be made and will foster innovation driven economy.

3. The signatories appreciate the initiatives developed by the project "Innovative Small and Medium Enterprises by Gender and Age" and basically support their implementation in Lithuania.

4. Committed support through the ongoing dialogue with all relevant stakeholder groups to create optimal conditions in the area of policy work, business, education, culture, social area, financial area aiming at increasing level of productivity and well- being of society.

5. Promoting gender- and age-management in the company for purpose of maintaining and strengthening the workability and the employability primarily of women and older people and improving productivity through wide-ranging information and advice services to SMEs.

6. Strong commitment to the comprehensive promotion of entrepreneurship in general and of companies created by women in particular, with the target to increase significantly the number of women entrepreneurs and start-ups to secure high economic stability and the opportunity to create additional jobs.

7. Education is the main key for fostering innovation, competitiveness and creation of more jobs. Therefore the signatories would like to promote education and training in general, as well as the development and approval of entrepreneurship education policy in Lithuania and the effective implementation of this policy.

8. It is obligated to create a web-based information platform online Forum, in which the parties which have signed the memorandum would be encouraged to participate in Forum discussions on current developments. It would be the basis for the discussions to shape the future of tactical activities and to provide the means to implement them. Women and older people's representatives would be an integral part of discussions in this online forum. Forum would be also useful to build and promote networking between women, older people and enterprises in association with nongovernmental organizations, which represents them.

Memorandum parties recognize its consultancy role and agree to voluntarily participate in online Forum discussions.

9. By undersigning the Memorandum we agree to work closely together at a strategic level in areas of common interest with the view to promoting innovations via equal opportunities for women and the development of women and older persons as employees and entrepreneurs in Lithuania.

10. Other institutions and organizations are invited to join this Memorandum and to take an active part in the important social, economic and political task to promote opportunities for women and older people in the SME sector in Lithuania.

Signatories:
- The Ministry of Economy of the Republic of Lithuania, Birutė Vėsaitė
- The Ministry of Social Security and Labor, Algimanta Pabėdinskienė
- The Ministry of Education and Science, Dainius Pavalkis
- Vilnius Gediminas Technical University, Alfonsas Daniūnas
- Lithuanian University of Educational Sciences, Algirdas Gaižutis
- Lithuanian Confederation of Industrialists Executive Authority CEO, Gediminas Rainys
- Lithuanian Women Association, Virginija Apanavičienė
- Labor and Social Research Institution, Boguslavas Gruževskis
- Vilnius Chamber of Commerce, Industry and Crafts, Vaclovas Kantrauskas
- Lithuanian Association of Local Authorities, Roma Žakaitienė (director)
- Panevėžys Chamber of Commerce, Industry and Crafts, Visvaldas Matkevičius

3.2.3   National Memorandum of Understanding of Poland

As the signatories of the memorandum, representatives the local government, non-governmental organizations, industry associations, public organizations, we recognize the current problematic situation and challenges faced by Poland, by signing this memorandum we commit to:

1. Supporting actions aimed at equality at work women and men, so that their full potential could be leveraged for the purpose of promoting creativity and know-how development.

2. Promotion of the sustainable employment of women and the elderly as enhancing their life quality. This employment has important impact upon the competitiveness of regional and national economy.

3. Engagement in the ongoing dialogue with all relevant stakeholder groups to create optimal conditions in the area of employment, business, education, culture and social policies.

4. Promoting wide access to information on gender- and age-management in organizations with the purpose of: strengthening the job activity primarily among women and the elderly and increasing the employability among SMEs.

5. Commitment to the promotion of entrepreneurship in general and, in particular, of companies created by women, in order to increase the number of women entrepreneurs and start-ups as well as to create additional work places.

6. Acknowledgment that education is the main key for fostering innovation, competitiveness and creation jobs. Therefore, the signatories would like to promote education and training in general, as well as the development and approval of entrepreneurship education policy and its effective implementation in Poland.

7. The signatories appreciate the initiatives developed by the project "Innovative Small and Medium Enterprises by Gender and Age" and as long as it is possible support their implementation in Poland.

8. By undersigning the Memorandum we agree to support all forms of cooperation aimed at the effective use of knowledge and experience of women and the elderly which enhance the competitiveness and innovativeness of SMEs on the regional, domestic and international level.

9. Other institutions and organizations are invited to join this Memorandum and to take an active part in the important social, economic and political task to promote opportunities for women and the elderly in the SME sector in Poland.

Signatories:
- Prezydent Miasta Białegostoku
- Wojewódzki Urząd Pracy w Białymstoku
- Białostocka Fundacja Kształcenia Kadr
- Izba Przemysłowo-Handlowa w Białymstoku
- Izba Rzemieślnicza i Przedsiębiorczości w Białymstoku
- Podlaskie Stowarzyszenie Właścicielek Firm - Klub Kobiet Biznesu
- Wydział Ekonomii i Zarządzania Uniwersytetu w Białymstoku

3.2.4   National Memorandum of Understanding of Belarus

As the signatories of the memorandum we recognize the current situation and challenges faced by Belarus, by signing this memorandum we commit to:

1. Supporting actions aimed at equality at work women and men, so that their full potential could be leveraged for the purpose of promoting creativity and know-how development.

2. Promotion of the sustainable employment of women and the elderly as enhancing their life quality. This employment has important impact upon the competitiveness of regional and national economy.

3. Engagement in the ongoing dialogue with all relevant stakeholder groups to create optimal conditions in the area of employment, business, education, culture and social policies.

4. Promoting wide access to information on gender- and age-management in organizations with the purpose of: strengthening the job activity primarily among women and the elderly and increasing the employability among SMEs.

5. Commitment to the promotion of entrepreneurship in general and, in particular, of companies created by women, in order to increase the number of women entrepreneurs and start-ups as well as to create additional work places.

6. Acknowledgment that education is the main key for fostering innovation, competitiveness and creation jobs. Therefore, the signatories would like to promote education and training in general, as well as the development and approval of entrepreneurship education policy and its effective implementation.

7. The signatories appreciate the initiatives developed by the project "Innovative Small and Medium Enterprises by Gender and Age" and as long as it is possible support their implementation in Belarus.

8. By undersigning the Memorandum we agree to support all forms of cooperation aimed at the effective use of knowledge and experience of women and the elderly which enhance the competitiveness and innovativeness of SMEs on the regional, domestic and international level.

9. Other institutions and organizations are invited to join this Memorandum and to take an active part in the important social, economic and political task to promote opportunities for women and the elderly in the SME sector in Belarus.

Signatories:
- Belarusian Chamber of Commerce and Industry
- Minsk Department of the Belarussian Chamber of Commerce and Industry
- Brest Department of the Belarusian Chamber of Commerce and Industry
- Gomel Branch of the Belarusian Chamber of Commerce and Industry
- Mogilev Branch of Belarusian Chamber of Commerce and Industry
- Brest State University
- Women organisation

3.2.5 National Memorandum of Understanding of Northern Germany

As the signatories of the memorandum we recognize the current situation and challenges and make the following arrangements for the overcoming thereof:

1. Marketable innovations in SMEs and the creation of equal opportunities for women and men at the place of employment have special priority. Sustainable promotion of employment of women and older persons should be connected with the strengthening of regional innovation, productivity and growth. In the

public interest all the activities are focused on the promotion of SMEs, which are the backbone of economy and society.

2. The increase of the employment quota of women and older persons is required so that they could stay in the working life longer, start an activity or become self-employed. With the promotion of employment, employability and entrepreneurship first of all of women and older persons we also constructively face the effects of the demographic change.

3. Strategies and measures developed in the project "Innovative Small and Medium Enterprises by Gender and Age" are supported according to current opportunities in order to achieve the implementation and continued use in the Northern Germany.

4. The international dialogue should be continued and intensified in order to learn from each other, to exchange experiences and to find further Best Practice solutions.

5. It requires an intensive public relation work and a broad dialogue in order to make the special benefits of women and older persons known and to inform of the chances for the development of the society and economy.

6. In the ongoing dialogue with all the relevant groups of actors the signatories commit themselves to the creation of optimal framework conditions in the field of political work, in economy, education, culture, social affairs and finances.

7. The promotion of gender and generation management at the enterprises is aimed at the preservation and strengthening of work ability and employability especially of women and older persons and also the improvement of productivity. Comprehensive information and consultation for SMEs should support this.

8. Especially intensive engagement is being developed for the comprehensive promotion of entrepreneurship in general as well as setting up business by women especially for the purpose to considerably increase the number of female entrepreneurs and to achieve setting up businesses with higher economic stability and the chance for the creation of additional working positions.+

9. Education is an important key factor for the promotion of innovations, competitive ability and creation of more working places. Further development of professional education and further education are actively supported including the promotion of women in so called "Male professions". The signatories firmly speak out in favour of rooting and sustainable promotion of entrepreneurship in the educational policy.

10. By signing the Memorandum we agree to cooperate at the strategic level in the fields of common interests for the promotion of equal opportunities of women and older persons as female employees and entrepreneurs. Further institutions and organizations are invited to join this Memorandum and to cooperate actively by the performance of the important social and economic task for the promotion of equal opportunities of women and older persons in the medium-sized enterprises of the Northern Germany.

Signatories:
- Hanse-Parlament
- Baltic Sea Academy
- Hamburgisches WeltWirtschaftsInstitut
- Handwerkskammer Schwerin
- Arbeit und Zukunft
- Verband Deutscher Unternehmerinnen, Landesverband Hamburg-Schleswig Holstein
- Verband Deutscher Unternehmerinnen, Landesverband Mecklenburg-Vorpommern

4. BSR-wide study of Best Practice support measures for women, elders and managers/owners of SMEs

4.1 The analysis of the conditions for best practices' transfer – Abstract

4.1.1 Introduction

In the report Grzesiak and Richert-Kaźmierska [Grzesiak, Richert-Kaźmierska 2013] focused on presenting the diagnosis methodology related to the possibilities and the conditions of selected good practices implementation in BSR countries adopted in the course of the research, as well as on discussing the obtained results. In this manual this report is partly presented[5].

One of the tasks of the Project Partners was identifying best practices in strengthening the economic activity of women and older people in the context of developing the competitiveness and innovation of SMEs, as well as determining the possibilities and conditions of their transfer. Transfer in this case is understood as the implementation of selected and described solutions in enterprises and public organizations from all the Baltic Sea Region (BSR) countries.

The coordination of the task and achieving the expected results of the project in this part was the responsibility of the Gdańsk University of Technology (PP10). Due to the complexity of the data analysis process (the data is often available only in the vernaculars) and the need to define specific conditions for the implementation of individual solutions in different countries, all project partners participated in performing the task[6].

---

[5] For the full report see Baltc Sea Academy Vol. 16 „Women and elderly on the BSR labour market - good practices' analysis and transfer",

[5] The exceptions were the Minsk and Brest Departments of the Belarusian Chamber of Commerce and Industry, which remained inactive in the project during the performance of the task due to formal reasons.

4.1.2 Research methodology

Enterprises and public organizations most often use best practices to attain satisfactory market position and ensure competitiveness cheaper and faster, as compared to the circumstances in which they would have to create specific solutions on their own. Searching for best practice which could be a model is usually a task of the concerned entity (enterprise or public organization) and results from a thorough self-assessment and benchmarking process[7]. More and more often, however, the best practices are subject to accreditation and the information about them is publicly available[8].

Transfer of best practices is one of the most difficult processes in the management of organizations. The solutions which proved effective in organization Y cannot be simply copied and implemented in organization X. It must be taken into account that the effect achieved by organization Y is affected by a number of its idiosyncratic circumstances, both dependent and independent of Y. Due to other circumstances and the internal structure of organization X, applying the same solutions and actions as in the case of organization Y may yield quite different results. Caution in the use of best practices results from the situational approach in management. Representatives of this perspective focus on the description and analysis of a variety of both internal and external conditions, the nature and interconnectedness of which justify the application of a given organizational model[9]. The basic premise of the situational approach is the relativism of the organizational rules and principles, i.e. assuming that they apply only in relation to certain categories of situations[10].

---

[6] Bogan, C.E. and English, M.J. (1994). Benchmarking for Best Practices: Winning Through Innovative Adaptation. New York: McGraw-Hill.

[7] Nash, J. and Ehrenfeld, J., 1997: Codes of environmental management practice: assessing their potential as a tool for change. Annual Review of Energy and the Environment 22.

[8] B. Kaczmarek, Cz. Sikorski, Podstawy zarządzania. Zachowania organizacyjne, Absolwent, Łódź 1998, p. 24.

[10] A. Stabryła, J. Trzcieniecki, Organizacja i zarządzanie. Zarys problematyki, Akademia Ekonomiczna w Krakowie, Kraków 1986, p. 183–184.

As reported by the American Productivity and Quality Centre, the main limitations for effective implementation of best practices in follower organizations are:[11]

- insufficient involvement of the management in the process of identifying best practices and their implementation,
- incorrect choice of the model solution, being unsuitable for a given problem,
- silo thinking and lack of mutual communication between the different departments of the organization,
- too short a time for learning the given best practice and the conditions for its success, as well as the fast pace of implementation and too high expectations regarding the quick development of positive effects,
- missing or insufficient experience of employees preventing or slowing down the effective implementation of a best practice.

Among the critical success factors of best practice transfer in enterprises, the professionals distinguish i.a. selecting an appropriate model solution, understanding the determinants of its effective implementation or ensuring favourable conditions for the implementation in the follower organization (see Table 1).

Table 1. Critical conditions of best practice implementation success

Related to the best practice chosen for implementation	• common goal of best practice and the implementing enterprise
	• appropriate choice, aligned with the implementing enterprise competences
Related to the workforce of the implementing enterprise	• suitable qualifications of the workforce enabling the implementation
	• proper selection of the team responsible for the implementation

---

[11]http://www.themanagementor.com/kuniverse/kmailers_universe/manu_kmailers/bp_ensurecomp3.htm

Related to the management of the implementing enterprise	• internal communication and promotion of best practice ideas
	• creating an environment conducive to the best practice being implemented and willing to share its expertise
	• providing the infrastructure necessary for the implementation
	• management commitment

Source: [Jarrar F.Y., Zairi M.,Best practice transfer for future competitiveness: A study of best practices.,Total Quality Management, 07/2000 in Grzesiak, Richert-Kaźmierska 2013, p. 5]

4.1.3 Selection of best practices

One of the areas of activity within the project was the selection of best practices related to strengthening the economic activity of women and seniors in the context of developing the competitiveness and innovation of SMEs. Due to the Scandinavian enterprises' considerable experience in this area, the best practices were sought among them with view to possible future implementation in the remaining BSR countries, mainly in Lithuania, Latvia, Germany and Poland.

A comprehensive analysis of the solutions used mainly by Scandinavian companies and public organizations to combine the economic activity of women and seniors with enterprise innovation, as well as complex consultations with other partners of the project, allowed GUT to select 11 best practices: 6 related to women's activity and 5 based on solutions used in the case of older workers (see Table 2). [see: Grzesiak, Richert-Kaźmierska 2013, p.6]

Table 2. Best practices selected for implementation

Focused on using the potential of women	Female future
	Women into Technology

	Pay Equity Action Plan
	Fuuturi: Women entrepreneurs and management future
	Women@Work
	Ambassadors for Women's entrepreneurship
Focused on using the potential of seniors	Senior policy in working life
	Senior enterprises – experience never ages
	Age management programme
	Flexible work practices
	Higher Vocational Education

Source: [Grzesiak, Richert-Kaźmierska 2013, p.6]

A short description of a couple of best practices selected as model solutions for implementation in remaining BSR countries is presented in chapter 4.2. of this manual.

4.1.4   Results of the research

In the analysis of the implementation conditions of selected best practices four categories were taken into account [Grzesiak, Richert-Kaźmierska 2013, p. 31]:

- financial issues, including the availability of aid from the European Union for the implementation of similar solutions,
- formal and legal issues,
- alignment of the best practice issues (economic activity of women and seniors in the context of developing innovation and competitiveness of SMEs) with the objectives and activities of the central, regional and local authorities and enterprises,
- readiness and commitment of public and private partners in the implementation process of the outlined best practices.

On the basis of the obtained answers it can be unequivocally stated that the risk of implementing any of the proposed solutions has been assessed as low (cf. Figures 43 and 45). In the case of best practices related to the economic activation of the seniors the practices recognized by respondents as burdened with high risk were "Senior enterprises – experience never ages" and "Senior policy in working life", whereas in the case of practices oriented towards the activation of women the most risky are "Pay Equity Action Plan" and "Female Future".

Figure 1. The risk of failure for seniors' practices is high – number of answers in total

Source: [Grzesiak, Richert-Kaźmierska 2013, p. 31]

Figure 2. The risk of failure for women's practices is high – number of answers in total

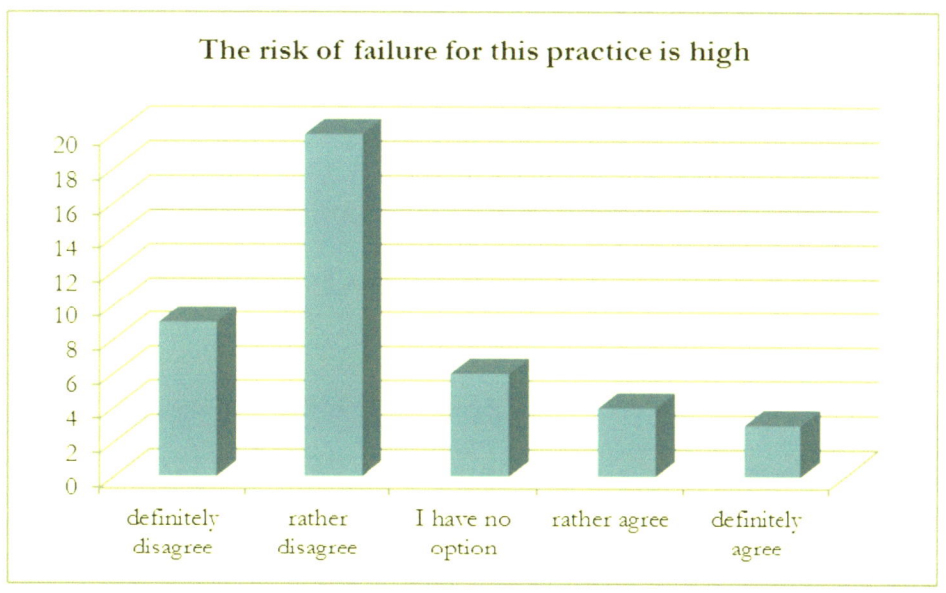

Source: [Grzesiak, Richert-Kaźmierska 2013, p. 32]

The results also allow for formulating some general conclusions (Source: [Grzesiak, Richert-Kaźmierska 2013, p. 33-34]):

- opportunities and conditions for the implementation of various best practices vary greatly due to their intrinsic characteristics,
- the efficiency of best practice implementation will be affected by the specificity of individual countries, and in particular by the level of public awareness — in this sense, the establishment of uniform guidelines regarding the implementation seems to be unfounded,
- one of the universal barriers (both in respect of the types of best practices and in respect of the country of implementation) is the shortage of own financial resources and low availability of external funds,
- a serious problem in the implementation of the proposed solutions may be related to the low public awareness of the need of economic activation of the groups hitherto traditionally marginalized in the labour market (mainly women

and seniors), as well as to linking the activation to building innovation and competitiveness of enterprises — studies suggest that such awareness is low, although higher in the case of women,

- although the respondents assessed the implementation of the proposed best practices as relatively poor, they also said that the implementing entities will probably not be able to count on the support of national and regional authorities,
- a barrier to the authority engagement in the implementation process may be their lack of experience, knowledge and skills,
- the formal and legal issues should not be an obstacle to the implementation of the proposed best practices,
- a key issue related to the implementation seems to be the low motivation of different types of entities to initiate the introduction of the proposed solutions.

4.2 Short description of best practices

In this part of manual selected part of the report concerning to the best practices transfer prepared by Grzesiak, Olczyk and Starnawska are presented. [Grzesiak, Olczyk, Starnawska 2013]

Female future mobilizing talents – a business perspective

The Confederation of Norwegian Enterprise (NHO) set up the Female Future project in 2003, and it lasted to 2008. It focused on this target group: Talented women working in private enterprises.

The goals of the project were: to increase the percentage of women in decision-making processes, in management and in boards in general; to cause that the private sector is viewed as an attractive place to work by women; to involve managers as prime movers in the process aimed at recruiting more women to executive positions and to board posts; to make executive responsibilities be more easily combined with family responsibilities - the balance between work and private life. The Female Future training program consists of three parts: Personal leadership training, Board competence and rhetoric. The training lasted from 13 to 15 days. In addition, throughout the duration of the project, selected women worked together with the managers of companies.

Last evaluation of the programme was done in May 2010: 62 % of the participants were offered board positions or advanced in their management career. The Female Future programme was appointed by ILO as one of the 10 best examples on Gender Equality.

Women into technology

Fife Women's Technology Centres (FWTC) were established in 1990 as a positive action initiative in order to train women who experienced real difficulty in obtaining work, so that they could rejoin the work force or take up further training opportunities. Their key priority was to widen horizons and raise aspirations by offering high quality training focussing on non-traditional areas, e.i. computing, electronics and IT.

The Programme "Women into Technology" started in year1992, which was aimed first of all at long term unemployed women, at lone parents, black and minority ethnic women, and women with disabilities. To be able to offer to the right path for entry into the labour market, the FWTC created the network of local partners.

WIT Core Programme covers 2,5 days per week over 48 weeks and consists of modules in maths, communication, technology and IT. The integrated part of this programme is the course of personal development, which covers to confidence building, assertiveness and team work.

The key success factors of training under WIT programme is the complex and integrated approach (materials, teaching methods), which guarantees a success path to the employment. Women, who took part in this project, indicated a supportive atmosphere connected with a high standard as a success factor.

FWTC won the Best Practice Award in ICT and was commended for the Equal Opportunities Award at the European Social Fund Objective 3 Awards.

Fuuturi: Women entrepreneurs and managers in the future

This project was a continuation of three earlier projects of the same aim but previously focused on women start-ups.

It started with a company Futuuri ('associated with the future') owned by a woman. This initiative ran between 2008 and2011 and focused on developing existing businesses owned by women. The project was implemented by North Savo Education (North Savo is a sparsely populated area in Finland), the University of Kuopio and the Savonia University of Applied Sciences.

The aims of the initiative were as follows:

- To promote women's entrepreneurship and management by speeding up the growth of enterprises and help the internationalization of the businesses, and also by supporting the participants' own business development projects.
- To develop the know-how and self-esteem of women entrepreneurs and managers has also been a goal. In addition, there has been a goal to develop each enterprise's knowledge-intensive service and product innovations.
- To support co-operation in networks among women.

Activities of the project included for example a course with teaching methods like lectures, discussions, and study trips built around seven separate modules. The women also participated in volunteer-based development circles where they could exchange ideas, also had opportunity to gain support from other women working in the same sector of the economy.

The results of the initiative were as following:

- 196 women entrepreneurs have taken part in the initiative;
- more than 100 company owners got to plan;
- longer scale strategies and visions;
- more than 200 women entrepreneurs or leaders made a development plan and put these plans in action;
- at least 5 new product or service innovations were made in these companies;
- at least 10 new theses about women's entrepreneurship were prepared.

Pay Equity Action Plan

Each year, employers must prepare a plan describing their efforts to promote gender equality. The plan shall contain a survey of different measures which are required at the workplace and shall indicate which of such measures the employer intends to initiate or implement during the coming year:

a) Working conditions: employers must take whatever steps may be required, insofar as their resources and general circumstances permit, to ensure that working conditions are suitable for both women and men.

b) Employers shall facilitate the combination of gainful employment and parenthood with respect to both female and male employees.

c) Employers shall take measures to forestall and prevent any employee from being subjected to gender-related harassment, to sexual harassment or to victimisation.

d) Recruitment, etc.: employers shall, through training, skills development and other suitable measures, promote an equal distribution between women and men in various types of work and within different categories of employees.

e) Employers shall endeavor to ensure that both women and men apply for vacant positions.

f) Employers are required to formulate a pay equity action plan in order to ensure that remuneration is fixed on the basis of objective criteria that are common to all jobs. The employer must take into account following criteria: qualifications, responsibilities, efforts and working conditions."

Women@Work (W@W)

Initiative providing training and information for women. It gives women skill development via a learning programme, more ability to express their concerns about gender issues at workplace, in families and communities where they live, use their full potential in these environments. This undertaking involves different bodies and industries. W@W has its own advisory group consisting of representatives from public, private and third sectors. W@W involves employed women who have job experience and also focuses on more isolated women as a result of living in rural areas.

- It provides forum where ideas and opinions are exchanged.
- Also, it supports women to share experiences via networking thus making contacts and growing in confidence.
- It promotes women leadership via trainings and consultation on national and international level.
- Organizes regular network meetings, speeches of guests, trainings and workshops.

Ambassadors for Women's entrepreneurship

This initiative is a part of Swedish National Programme to Promote Women's Entrepreneurship. Women Ambassadors are meant to work as role models to raise the interest about entrepreneurship, so that younger women t consider running a business as a career choice. The dominant image of a man as a picture of a small business owner-manager is aimed to be changed via this initiative Ambassadors make attempts to disseminate the knowledge about entrepreneurship and also contribute to rise the interest of public media in women entrepreneurship issue.

Being ambassador carries:

- doing four voluntary jobs per year, such as speaking at different educational institutions such as schools or universities,
- doing study visits or hold personal meetings with women considering business start-up.

Each ambassador is provided with a toolbox with all the useful materials to perform ambassadorial visit. Ambassadors organize visits to their companies, do work shadowing, offer business training as well as mentoring. Such ambassadors make an important mark in business and society as role models as they their stories and experiences. The ambassadors refer to different aspects of entrepreneurship, and so more women might consider themselves as entrepreneurs.

The ambassadors are varied in terms of the businesses they represent. They are located all over the country. Each Swedish county (official admin. region) has between 15-40 ambassadors. Cities like Stockholm, Göteborg and Malmö have more ambassadors than the rest of the counties.

Other activities and measures in the whole programme include:

- Providing information, business advice, business development
- Running actions regarding business transfer
- Providing mentorship
- Supporting entrepreneurship among women academics
- Developing financing opportunities

Senior policy in working life

Senior policy in working life is based on a strategy of cooperation between relevant government agencies, major unions and employer's associations and other professionals. The aims, and the most essential means, are presented in National Initiative for Senior Workers in Norway and The Tripartite Agreement on a more Inclusive Workplace – a contract signed up by the government and social partners.

CSP is responsible for coordinating the National Initiative. The Initiative was taken in order to discourage older workers from taking early retirement and promote a longer working career. The target group are workers from the age of 45-50. The Initiative is part of the strategy aimed at top management of all the major unions, employers' associations and relevant government agencies. In brief, the Initiative consists of the following:

- Promote awareness of the potentials and resources older employees hold.
- Provide a better and more inclusive working environment for all workers.

Create more cooperation among labour, employer and government organizations and authorities concerning senior policy. The Tripartite Agreement on a more Inclusive Workplace is an initiative supported by the Government and its social partners to encourage people with different hindrances for employment, such as disability, early retirement pension or sickness benefits, to return to work, at least part time. The agreement, which lasted from October 2001 to 31 December 2005, had three objectives, which match the intention of the senior policy:

- Reduce sick leave by at least 20 % by the end of the agreement period.
- Increase significantly employment among those that have minor disabilities.
- Increase the average age at which seniors choose to retire.

The aim is to achieve these objectives through voluntary agreements between company-level employers and the National Insurance Authority, with CSP as an important coordinator. To this end, the Centre has worked out a national plan in cooperation with the social partners to make individuals, companies and politicians aware of the advantages of hiring and retaining workers over the age of 45. The majority of the senior policy initiatives are focused on promoting good personnel policy in general and create a more accommodating workplace. Senior policy is based upon experiences that show that personnel policy initiatives and other developing methods must have a life span perspective. Preventive efforts must therefore begin early in a person's career.

<u>Senior enterprises – experience never ages</u>

There are four main areas of the initiative:

- providing the knowledge and building the awareness - mainly training for people aged 50+ diagnosing and presenting the possibilities of their professional development, including starting the own business; distribution of information about tools available for new business owners – start-up's supporting system;
- substantive and organizational support for those persons 50+ who decide to start their own business including assistance in finding partners (training, financial assistance, a database of potential business partners);
- maintain the database of individuals aged 50 + interested in investing their funds in new business (Business Angels);
- cooperation with people 50 +: entrepreneurs, professionals in various fields of business, interested in providing advisory services (mentoring) for new entrepreneurs, including those aged 50 + (group and individual meetings with counsellors).

Rising awareness' activities are addressed to three main target groups:

- those aged 50+ to present the possibilities given by the initiative;
- enterprise development agencies, financial institutions, agencies working with older people, younger entrepreneurs to show up the untapped potential that exists among older people;

- policy maker to convince them (politicians on different levels) to the idea of 50+ engagement in economy.

Starting and partnering activities deliver support instruments, which help older persons to start their new business (by themselves or in partnership with younger ones). The initiative supports older individuals to explore the personal, financial and commercial aspects involved in taking the first step into entrepreneurship. Those aged 50+ may consider starting a business in partnership with a younger individual. The drive and enthusiasm of the younger person would then benefit from the wider knowledge, experience, networks and resources of the older individual.

Investing and acquiring, those are activities focused on "using" the finances of successful 50+, who represent an excellent potential source of investment. In many respects the most rewarding form of investment is when an individual aged 50+ invests in a business sector that he/she knows well and brings expertise, as well as money, to the new business (star-up).

Advising area is very important part of the initiative. Suitably qualified and experienced older people provide the support to owner managers of new and existing businesses. They share with their knowledge and experience with the youngers and help them in designing strategic plans for their companies development.

Flexible work practices

Kronoberg County Council's most important responsibility relates to health care, and around 85 % of its activity is devoted to medical and health services. The council represents the largest employer in the county of Kronoberg, with 5,280 employees, 80 % of whom are women. The five largest staff categories are nurses (28 %), assistant nurses (15 %), doctors (9 %), keepers (9 %) and administrators (8 %). Employees' average age is 47 years. Almost 20 % of the workforce is aged between 50 and 59 years, almost 28 % are over 55 years and more than 11 % are aged over 60 years. The council expects many employees to retire within 10 years. Staff turnover is currently 6.7 %.

The main problem in personnel policy recognized by the council is that 40 % of health care employees will leave the labour market within 15 years. Therefore, the council depends on its older employees for both skills and staffing.

Presented initiative includes:

- skills training for managers – a plan for manager training is being prepared to ensure that the original initiative is implemented in everyday activities;
- using pensioners as substitutes–employees at two of the council's facilities can continue to work as substitutes after retirement when they reach 64 years of age;
- career planning at 55 years of age;
- mentorship – one of the council's facilities has a structured skills-transfer programme;
- enhancing workers' employability – the county council aims to keep all workers' skills up to date to preserve their employability;
- learning centre – the council has set up local learning centres that use modern techniques and where workers can pursue formal education or other training, flexibly and at their own pace;
- validation – the council plans to validate experience-based knowledge so that workers can more easily move between job categories or employers;
- career and advice centre – the council plans to set up a career and advice centre to facilitate career planning.

Higher Vocational Education

Higher vocational programme may be of 200 vocational credits (equivalent to one full academic year) or 400 vocational credits, corresponding to two full academic years. Swedish National Agency is responsible for allocation of funds on this type of education in Sweden.

Actually 1100 courses like this in Sweden, realized by different types of educational organizations (Sensus runs only one course – International Key Account Manager). Procedure in preparing the Higher Vocational Education Programme:

- steering group (different regional stake holders e.g. entrepreneurs, representatives of local authorities, representatives of trade unions etc.) execute the analysis of regional labour market's situation, especially in the field of scarce occupations;
- teachers, coachers, mentors and trainers in the course – high level specialists, practitioners from different types of institutions;
- programme aim – formation mainly practical high professional skills;
- educational organization interested in running such a course must apply for funds to Swedish National Agency – one application for two editions of the course;
- course group – 30-35 persons;
- courses last 2-4 semesters (10 hours of classes per week + own projects work + learning in work environment).

Higher Vocational Education Programmes result: more, needed on regional labour market, very high qualified specialists, ready to take over the management responsibility.

For further information, see: Gdansk University of Technology.

5. Results and experiences from the Train the Trainer programme and the training and coaching programme for consultants

5.1 Train the Trainer/Train the Consultant – Curricula and trainer's manual

Introduction

Train the Trainer and Train the Consultant training and coaching programmes have been planned in the QUICK-IGA project Innovative SMEs by Gender and Age. The aim of the QUICK-IGA training programmes is to improve advisory competences on improving work structures in SMEs to increase labour participation of women and elders and innovation capacities.

Train the Trainer programme is planned for the professional teaching staff of academies, universities and further education institutions. Train the Consultant programme is planned for the professional teaching staff of academies and universities, consultants from chambers of commerce, crafts, SME promoters, and women organizations and elderly employee organizations.

Both training programmes provide participants with necessary background information about the current situation of women and elderly employers in the European Union area, means to tackle the obstacles of women's and elderly person's employability, best practices and case studies, and the pedagogical issues related to the organization of the training courses. The duration of the Train the Trainer course is one day, and the Train the Consultant course 1 - 2 days.

The curriculum of both training courses is quite flexible, and each organizer can focus the content to meet the needs of their own participants. Thus, the manual contains links to suggested statistical materials, best practices, reports and case studies. Country specific information should be included by organizers themselves. The main objective of the courses is to give participants necessary skills, knowledge and tools to reinforce the positive development of women's and elderly person's employability. The teaching methods used should include sharing knowledge on best practices and participant's own experiences. Suggested course feedback questions are also given. After the training the participants will be given certificates. Models for both training course certificates are also attached to this manual.

The training courses have been implemented as follows:

- Train the Trainer courses in Vilnius, Lithuania 20.9.2012 and in Bialystok, Poland 13.9.2013
- Training the Consultant courses in Brest, Belarus 26.10.2012, in Gdansk, Poland 7.-8.3.2013 and in Riga, Latvia 19.- 20.9.2013

Course feedbacks have been collected from all the courses organized. The analysis of the feedbacks is available in the publication Quick-IGA, Train the Trainer, Train the Consultant, Feedbacks, 2013.

The Train the Trainer course will be transferred to 15 universities from nine BSR countries (Member of Baltic Sea Academy), and the Train the Consultant course to 50 Chambers from 11 BSR countries (Members of Hanse-Parlament).

5.2 QUICK-IGA Train the Trainer curricula

5.2.1 Target Groups and Learning Outcomes

Train the Trainer programme is planned for the professional teaching staff of academies, universities and further education institutions.

Learning outcomes include that the participants are ready to train, coach and qualify staff of chambers, associations and other institutions on women and elderly person employment. After the training participants possess the necessary skills and knowledge related to planning and organizing effective training in empowerment of women and elderly persons.

Core contents include the key aspects on the European and country wise demographic trends, employment, job structure, and social situation, tackling the contextual, economic and soft obstacles of women and elderly person's innovative employability, pedagogical principles of organizing effective training courses.

5.2.2   Technical Unit 1

Technical Unit 1: **Key figures on the European demographic trends, employment, job structure and social situation**

Introductory lecture on Key figures on the European demographic trends, employment job structure and social situation. The content of the lecture includes economic, employment and social implications of demographic trends, demographic revolution, labour market and sector challenges, productivity growth, changes in job structures, patters of employment shift by gender and age, enhancing women and elderly person's involvement in economic growth and productivity, skills supply and demand, labour market participation policies, active ageing strategies and measures, entrepreneurship.

Useful links related to the statistics and Technical Unit 1:

- Eurostat website pages aim to be the leading provider of high quality statistics in Europe and its Member States. Related to the topics in this manual the themes *Economy and finance*, *Population and social conditions*, *Industry, trade and services*, *Environment and energy*, and *Science and technology* might bring some relevant information.
  http://epp.eurostat.ec.europa.eu/portal/page/portal/statistics/themes

- This specific page from Eurostat is about the gender pay gap
  http://epp.eurostat.ec.europa.eu/statistics_explained/index.php/Gender_pay_gap_statistics

- Report by European Commission about the statistics in different Member States. Wes - the European network to promote women's entrepreneurship activities report.
  http://ec.europa.eu/enterprise/policies/sme/promoting-entrepreneurship/women/wes-network/

- Statistical information about the differences between women and men during their lives from working years to pensions. The life of women and men in Europe report.

  http://epp.eurostat.ec.europa.eu/cache/ITY_OFFPUB/KS-80-07-135/EN/KS-80-07-135-EN.PDF

- Employment trends and policies for older people in the recession report has data on recent employment trends for older workers in the EU27.
  http://www.eurofound.europa.eu/pubdocs/2012/35/en/1/EF1235EN.pdf

- Women Entrepreneurs in the OECD describes key evidence and policy challenges.
  http://www.oecd-ilibrary.org/social-issues-migration-health/women-entrepreneurs-in-the-oecd_5k43bvtkmb8v-en

5.2.3   Technical Unit 2

Technical Unit 2: **Tackling the contextual, economic and soft obstacles of women and elderly person's innovative employability**

Lecture on tackling the contextual, economic and soft obstacles of women and elderly person's innovative employability. The content of the lecture includes education choices, traditional views and stereotypes about women and elderly and innovation, women's and elderly person's credibility, lack of access to professional networks, lack of business training, role model, leadership and management skills, promotion of female and elderly employability and entrepreneurship, innovation and productivity increase with women and elderly.

Useful links to Technical Unit 2:

Women

- Evaluation Policy: Promotion of Women innovators and entrepreneurship-report from the European Commission page deals with the different kind of obstacles that prevent women to enter the business world. It has also information about the Member States countrywide.
  http://ec.europa.eu/enterprise/dg/files/evaluation/women_en.pdf

- The European Commission web-page about promoting women entrepreneurs in small and medium-sized enterprises (SMEs)

  http://ec.europa.eu/enterprise/policies/sme/promoting-entrepreneurship/women/

- Enterprising Women, Great-Britain women entrepreneurs, national organization's web page. http://www.enterprising-women.org/

- YouTube video: Euronews business planet; Boosting women entrepreneurs http://www.youtube.com/watch?v=M7StuuqDl80&list=TLFGAwsbMymHlUY-Pp3ZAXlS8_SPm7xSje

- Break gender stereotypes –report is a toolkit for SME Advisors and Human Resource Managers to break gender stereotypes and give talents a change http://www.businessandgender.eu/en/products/toolkit-for-sme-advisors-and-human-resource-managers

- A study of collected narratives on gender perceptions in the 27 EU Member States http://eige.europa.eu/sites/default/files/EIGE-study-on-collected-narratives-on-gender-perceptions-MH3112337ENC.pdf

- Web page from European Commission having many reports and links about the equality between women and men. http://europa.eu/legislation_summaries/employment_and_social_policy/equality_between_men_and_women/

- European Commission's strategy for equality between men and women 2010-2015 http://europa.eu/legislation_summaries/employment_and_social_policy/equality_between_men_and_women/em0037_en.htm and http://epp.eurostat.ec.europa.eu/statistics_explained/index.php/Gender_pay_gap_statistics

- Family life and work report summarizes issues related to the family and work. It has sections dealing the work - family balance, working time etc. in Europe Union. https://osha.europa.eu/en/publications/e-facts/e-fact-57-family-issues-work-life-balance

Older workers

- Workplace age discrimination is the most frequently reported form of age discrimination. Active Ageing - report from the webpage https://osha.europa.eu/en/priority_groups/ageingworkers/index_html

- Report: The Impact of the Crises on Senior Workers: Challenges and Responses by PES http://www.mobilitypartnership.eu/Documents/EJML%20Senior%20workers%20final.pdf

- Website of the Age Platform Europe promote the interest of seniors. http://www.age-platform.eu/index.php

- Website of Ageing workers by European Agency for Safety and Health at work has wide discussion about older people at work and how to promote older people and about active ageing. https://osha.europa.eu/en/priority_groups/ageingworkers/index_html

5.2.4 Technical Unit 3

Technical Unit 3: **Pedagogical principles of planning and organizing effective training course**

Lecture on Pedagogical principles of planning and organizing effective training courses. The content of the lecture includes principles of organizing training courses, target group analysis, pedagogical approaches and technical strategies, attitude awareness and motivation, involving participants, traditional lectures, making lectures more interesting, i.e. inserting visual elements like examples, illustrations, figures, tables, videos, Internet sites, etc., case methods, discussions forums, role plays, drama, pedagogy, simulations, coaching, mentoring, individual and group activities, e-learning, use of knowledge bases, leaning from best practices and worst cases, professional visits, course feed-back, further development.

There are plenty of different kind of documents and reports about how to improve the training sessions. There will be more information about the content of this Technical Unit in the section Learning Methods.

5.2.5 Course Feedback

There will be a feedback form for the participants to fill in after the course has ended. The subject of the evaluation is

1) the course itself with all the Technical Units
2) the framework conditions out of the course: lecturers, organization, materials etc.

This evaluation of the course was carried out to check the whole course, to reveal eventual weaknesses or to incorporate new aspects.

The actual feedback form will be in the Annex 1.

5.2.6 Certificate

All participants will receive a certificate for their forward participation after the course has ended.

5.3 QUICK-IGA Train the Consultant curricula

5.3.1 Target Group and Learning Outcomes

Train the Consultant programme is planned for the professional teaching staff of academies and universities, consultants from chambers of commerce, crafts, SME promoters, and women organizations and elderly employee organizations.

Learning outcomes include that the participants are ready to coach and mentor female entrepreneurs and elderly entrepreneurs. After the training participants poses the necessity skills and knowledge to guide females and elderly to run successful businesses in practice, to increase productivity, and to create innovation capacity in SME's.

Core contents include the key aspects on the Baltic Sea Region and country wise demographic trends, employment, job structure and social situation women and elderly person's employability, increasing productivity, creation of innovation capacity, special leadership and management skills needed with women and elderly, organizing effective consultations, communication and crises management.

5.3.2 Technical Unit 1

Technical Unit 1: **Key figures on the Baltic Sea Region demographic trends, employment, job structure and social situation**

Lecture on Key figures on the Baltic Sea region demographic trends, employment, and job structure social situation. The content of the lecture includes employment and social implications of demographic trends, demographic revolution, labour market and sectorial changes, productivity growth changes in job structures, patterns of employment shift by gender and age, enhancing women and elderly person's involvement in economic growth and productivity, skills supply and demand, labour market participation policies, active ageing strategies and measures, entrepreneurship.

- The demographic trends of Baltic Sea Region and its members can be found from Eurostat pages, which aim to be the leading provider of high quality statistics in Europe and its Member States. Related to the topics in this manual the themes *Economy and finance*, *Population and social conditions*, *Industry, trade and services*, *Environment and energy*, and *Science and technology* might bring some relevant information.
  http://epp.eurostat.ec.europa.eu/portal/page/portal/statistics/themes

- Specific information about the Member States and their situation with gender issues can be also found from the report Promotion of Women Innovators and Entrepreneurs.
  http://ec.europa.eu/enterprise/newsroom/cf/_getdocument.cfm?doc_id=3815

5.3.3 Technical Unit 2

Technical Unit 2: **Increasing productivity and creation of innovation capacity in SMEs**

Lecture on Increasing productivity and creation of innovation capacity in SME's. The content of the lecture includes attracting women and elderly persons in SME's, breaking traditional views and stereotypes about women and elderly, SME's expectations of productive employees, increasing SMEs innovation and productivity by employing women and elderly persons, leadership and management and organizational development in strengthening the productivity of SMEs, creativity and use of new knowledge capturing tacit knowledge, special advantages/benefits and disadvantages related to the employment of women and elderly persons.

Useful links related to the Technical Unit 2:

- European small business portal has gathered together all the information provided by the EU for SMEs, ranging from practical advice to policy issues. http://ec.europa.eu/small-business/index_en.htm

Women

- Equality between women and men -report from European Commission. The report is from the Eurostat web page. http://epp.eurostat.ec.europa.eu/statistics_explained/index.php/Gender_pay_gap_statistics

- Women in economic decision-making in the EU: Progress report deals with the questions of women in the leadership positions. (Women on boards) http://ec.europa.eu/justice/gender-equality/files/women-on-boards_en.pdf

- European Commission website on Small and medium-sized enterprises (SMEs) and encouraging women entrepreneurs. Website collects also links to National organizations of women entrepreneurs, International organizations of women entrepreneurs etc. http://ec.europa.eu/enterprise/policies/sme/promoting-entrepreneurship/women/index_en.htm

- Website of Business and Gender has much valuable information about the gender stereotypes and the benefits on breaking the stereotypes. They have also good videos promoting women and having good best practices. http://www.businessandgender.eu/en/home

- Break gender stereotypes, give talent a chance report offers information and practical guidance on the problems of SME's tackling with the stereotype problems and getting full potential on their employees both women and men. http://www.businessandgender.eu/splash

Older workers

- Promoting lifelong learning for older workers report has a wide overview of older people in working life and gives information and case examples about senior workers in different situations at their life and work.
http://www.cedefop.europa.eu/EN/Files/3045_en.pdf

- Demography, active ageing and pensions report focuses on the solutions to face the unavoidable change in the age structure and the growth of the number of older people and workers. The report concentrates also to the companies tackling with this change of the workers age structure.
http://ec.europa.eu/social/main.jsp?catId=738&langId=en&pubId=6805

- It's Time to Manage Age report proposes several solutions to turn population ageing into an opportunity for employers and companies, and to create greater solidarity and awareness on age diversity within the society.
http://www.adecco.com/en-US/Industry-Insights/Documents/mature_workers_2011.pdf

5.3.4   Technical Unit 3

Technical Unit 3: **Tackling to the consultation needs of women and elderly**

Lecture on tackling to the consultation needs of women and elderly. The content of the lecture includes age management policies, attitude awareness, support self-confident, increasing credibility, development of positive organizational culture, special employee obligations to be met with women and elderly, employment services, well-being of women and elderly people, consultation and needs of women and elderly persons, consultation of women entrepreneurs starting their business.

Useful material related to the Technical Unit 3:

- The Emerge of Age Management in Europe –article deals with the recent rise of interest in age management in personal and organizational level. The main focus areas are: "workforce ageing, the age/employment paradox, the public policy imperatives, the organizational pressures and the goal of equal opportunities or age diversity". (Walker 2004)

http://www.usq.edu.au/extrafiles/business/journals/HRMJournal/Internati
onalArticles/Volume10Ageing/WalkerVol10-1.pdf

- European Employment Observatory Review Employment Policies to
  Promote

- Active Ageing 2012 report has data from different EU Member States and
  their practices with older workers to promote active ageing in their
  communities and companies.
  http://ec.europa.eu/social/main.jsp?catId=738&langId=en&pubId=6805&t
  ype=2&furtherPubs=no

- Work-Related Health in Europe: Are Older People More at Risk? is a
  discussion paper, which examines whether the older workers differ a lot from
  younger workers. The discussion concentrates mostly on job related health
  risk perception, mental and physical health, sickness absence, probability of
  reporting injury and fatigue of older people. http://ftp.iza.org/dp6044.pdf

- PES (Public Employment Services) from European Commission has a PES
  and older workers report from a Peer Review that dealt with the aims of the
  Europe 2020 Strategy by enhancing the employability of older workers and
  removing barriers to their labour market participation. The report
  summarises the main issues discussed in the meeting including wide range of
  problems and challenges in older workers work life.
  http://ec.europa.eu/social/main.jsp?catId=964

5.3.5   Technical Unit 4

Technical Unit 4: **Organizing effective consultations**

Lecture on organizing effective consultations. The content of the lecture includes
appropriate consultation forms, mentoring and coaching, utilization of role models,
spreading best practices, learning from the worst cases, effective communication and
crises management, developing materials and documents for consultation of different
target groups.

- International organization concentrated to promote business and professional women.
  http://www.bpw-europe.org/

5.3.6 Course Feedback

There will be a feedback form for the participants to fill in after the course has ended. The subject of the evaluation is

1) the course itself with all the Technical Units
2) the framework conditions out of the course: lecturers, organization, materials etc.

This evaluation of the course was carried out to check the whole course, to reveal eventual weaknesses or to incorporate new aspects.

The feedback model questions will be in the Annex 1.

5.3.7 Certificate

All participants will receive a certificate for their forward participation after the course has ended.

5.4 Learning methods

There are a range of exercises the trainer can effectively use in order to involve in the participants as much as possible to the learning process. The best way for adults to learn is when the new course material is based on their experiences, but when there is also left space for the debate among the participants. There are varieties of training methods and together they can give the possibility for a multifaceted understanding of the course material.

Different kind of teaching methods are:

- "Auditory" methods, such as discussions, lectures, using tapes
- "Visual" methods, such as films and other demonstrative processes/tools
- "Physical" methods, such as role playing, group exercises or other physical exercises

The Trainer's Survival Guide has 25 different activities that make lecture-based programmers more active. They can be used during the training session and they have tips for the trainer to get participants involved.
http://www.leotrainer.com/tactiveteach.pdf

5.4.1 Icebreakers

In the beginning of the session it is important to get participants involved and engaged in an activity that requires them to talk and cooperate with the others. *Icebreakers* are the simple activities used at the beginning of a session to help participants learn each other's names and/or backgrounds, share their experiences, or introduce the topic of the lecture. The right icebreaker can help to get a positive and enjoyable learning experience for both the trainer and the participants. During the icebreakers participants should connect with at least one other person. Icebreakers should be topic related and at low risk so that participants would feel comfortable and easy. Time used for icebreakers should not be too long compared to the length of the session.

- The Assistive Technology Trainer's Handbook is a toolkit for assistive technology training and it offers wide range of information related to the training sessions, for example icebreakers, presentations, brainstorming etc.
  http://www.natenetwork.org/manuals-forms/at-trainers-handbook

- Creative Icebreakers, Introductions, and Hellos for Teachers, Trainers, and Facilitators –manual has 15 ideas for icebreaking in the beginning of trainer's session.
  http://www.businesstrainingworks.com/training-resources/free-icebreakers

5.4.2 Lectures

Presentation

The presentation (e.g. PowerPoint™ or Prezi (Prezi.com)) is used to support the content of the training and thus it should be clear and easy to read. The presentation is designed to be a visual support for both the trainer and the participants.

- Assistive Technology Trainer's Handbook
  http://www.natenetwork.org/manuals-forms/at-trainers-handbook

- Presentation Skills Training Resources and Articles
  http://www.businesstrainingworks.com/training-resources/presentation-skills-articles

Figures, Tables and Videos

In order to improve the attractiveness of the lecture and the presentation it would be advisable to include figures or tables or videos into the presentation/ the lecture. Figures and tables illustrate the situations well and thus make it easier for the participants to assimilate the gained information. Presentations of success stories and case studies can be also included to this section. Internet and Youtube offer good opportunity for researching suitable videos.

- Training of Trainers manual information and guidelines for making training sessions, they have also good information on figures and tables.
  http://hcfp.gov.in/downloads/manuals/Training_of_Trainers_Manual.pdf

- Example of a video that could be added to this specific topic (women and elderly in workplaces) featuring the stories of Ireland's SME which have enhanced their performance by breaking gender stereotypes:
  http://www.youtube.com/watch?feature=player_embedded&v=Qv8eWge8cu0

5.4.3   Group Work and Brainstorming

Group works can be applied in learning if the trainer wants participants to deal about the issue by debating and discussing. Group work in small groups gives all the participants the opportunity to participate in the exercises and thus express their ideas. In order to get the best out of the group works would be good to get them goal-oriented. The participants should understand the task of the group work at hand, the time-frame and the way of presenting the results.

- Trainer's Handbook
  http://hcfp.gov.in/downloads/manuals/Training_of_Trainers_Manual.pdf

Brainstorming involves the trainer ask an open-ended question and the participants to come up with as many solutions as possible. The idea of brainstorming is to get participants involved and engaged in the training. Brainstorming should be based on few rules in order to get the best results. Example of the rule could be that there are no stupid or bad ideas.

- Trainer's Handbook, Assistive Technology Trainer's handbook
  http://www.natenetwork.org/manuals-forms/at-trainers-handbook

5.4.4   Mentoring

Mentoring can be described as partnership between two people working in a same field or sharing same experiences. A mentor is a person helping the mentee to develop solutions to career related issues. Mentors should be helpful and get the mentee to believe in her while boosting her confidence. A good mentor also challenges and questions her mentee, but in the meantime provides guidance and encouragement. The most important meanings of mentoring are to enable others become more self-aware, to make them take responsible for their life and to direct their life in the direction they decide.

- Information on business mentoring, successful mentorship and the benefits of mentoring can be found from the Website
  http://www.micromentor.org/resources/resource-center

- YouTube video example on women mentors
  http://www.youtube.com/watch?v=DQBVDYFwiGY&list=UUvhco_i3akl_yhKLgsjEcNA&index=4&feature=plcp

5.4.5   Best Practices and Worst Case Scenarios

Best practices can be defined as "practices that consistently show results superior to those achieved with other means". (European Commission report on best practices p.17) Best practice examples can be used as a support and example during the training session. Good examples can be found from the document Europe can do better, Best practices for reducing administrative burdens.

- The webpage to European Commission best practices
  http://ec.europa.eu/dgs/secretariat_general/admin_burden/best_practice_report/best_practice_report_en.htm

- Case study, Best practices: P.E.O.P.L.E.
  The Pan European Older Person's Learning & Employment (P.E.O.P.L.E.) network funded by the EU Leonardo Da Vinci programme. The objective of this project was to develop a best practice network, research, education and communications system between EU partner organisations who are addressing the issues of ageism and promoting the interests of older working age people (50-65+), particularly in relation to education, training and employment. There are also four best practice guides for older people.
  http://www.wiseowls.co.uk/welcome/index/people_info

  The P.E.O.P.L.E webpage
  http://www.europeanpeoplenetwork.eu/

- Best practice on a project called AgeMasters in Finnish company Abloy.
  http://www.abloy.com/en/abloy/abloycom/About-ABLOY/Environmental-Responsibility/Age-Masters/

- EIGE (European Institute for Gender Equality) page has a lot material on gender issues http://eige.europa.eu/ and mainstreaming http://eige.europa.eu/content/activities/gender-mainstreaming-methods-and-tools

  YouTube video promoting women in companies from EIGE's website
  http://www.youtube.com/watch?feature=player_embedded&v=LQURPrp7xZQ

- Case study, Best practice: SLIC-project (lifelong learning for older workers)
  SLIC was a two-year project funded by the European Commission's GRUNDTVIG sub programme of the Lifelong Learning programme and led by the Austrian Red Cross, with partners based in organizations from Austria, Hungary, Germany, Italy, Finland and the UK. The aim was to develop new practical ways to help older adults review their past experience

and personal skills and explore new and potential opportunities for learning and community engagement.
http://www.slic-project.eu/trainingpf/slic2toolkit/index.php

Worst Case Scenarios can be defined as "worst possible environment or outcome out of the several possibilities in planning or simulation" (BusinessDictionary.com) During the training session worst cases can be helpful to the participants in order to help their planning of the future expenditure cuts and contingency in their businesses.

- Link behind the definition:
  http://www.businessdictionary.com/definition/worst-case-scenario.html

5.5   Training course concepts for future use

5.5.1   Train the Trainer course programme

In the future Train the Trainer courses will be organized by the universities and higher education institutes that are members of the Baltic Sea Academy. These training institutions will be qualified, and they will train the trainers to be able to train the consultants. The Baltic Sea academy members will also be responsible for the further development of the Train the Trainer course. The implementation of the course will ensure the sustainable qualification of trainers in the entire Baltic Sea Region.

Baltic Sea Academy institutions can create their own training packages based on this manual and the curricula. Some lecture material has been given in Annex 4. The useful list of material will give further material to address the expectations training groups may have. Every education event is of course independent, and the content of the course and their unit weight is to be fixed according to the needs of the target group. In all courses the experiences form a real working life and companies should be included. Sharing knowledge and experiences with the companies highlights well the current situation with women and elderly workers. During group activities possible solutions for the acute changes could be developed. Every organizer should distribute new training material through the Baltic Sea Academy electronic platform.

The finance of the Train the Trainer course could be arranged through registration fees. If local public support is available that could be used, too.

The daily programme for the Train the Trainer course is as follows:

Duration: 1 day

Programme

9:00	Welcome address Introduction to the Train the Trainer Curricula Short Presentation of the participants and their expectations
9:30	Introductory Lecture on **Key figures on the European demographic trends, employment, job structure and social situation**
10:15	Break (coffee/tea)
10:30	Lecture on **Tackling the contextual, economic and soft obstacles of women and elderly person's innovative employability**
12:00	Lunch break
13:00	Lecture on **Pedagogical principles of planning and organizing effective training courses**
14:00	Break (coffee/tea)
14:15	Group activity on pedagogical approaches
16:00	Wrap-up and evaluation of the Train the Trainer course
16:30	Closing words

5.5.2   Train the Consultant Course Programme

The qualified trainers of all participating universities and higher education institutes will continuously coach and train consultants, which give advice to SMEs, women, and elderly. These consultants work in chambers, other SME promoters, educational institutions, public administrations or other relevant consultancies. This ensures that trainings and consulting can be implemented on a permanent basis. An increasing number of consultants with will be qualified, who in turn will support SMEs, women and elders and, thus, will promote a broadening the innovation basis of SMEs.

All organizers can create their own training packages based on this manual and the curricula. Some lecture material has been given in Annex 5, 6 and 7. The useful list of material will give further material to address the expectations training groups may have. Every education event is of course independent, and the content of the course and their unit weight is to be fixed according to the needs of the target group. In all courses the experiences form a real working life and companies should be included. Sharing knowledge and experiences with the companies highlights well the current situation with women and elderly workers. All participants should be challenged to the innovation capacity development. Every training course should have at least one visit to a company. Every organizer should distribute new training material through the Baltic Sea Academy electronic platform.

The finance of the Train the Consultant course could be arranged through registration fees. If local public support is available that could be used, too.

The daily programmes for the Train the Consultant is as follows:

Duration: 1 – 2 days

Day 1 Programme

9:00   Welcome address
               Introduction to the Train the Consultant Curricula
               Short presentation of the participants and their expectations

9:30	Introductory Lecture on **Key figures on the Baltic Sea Region demographic trends, employment, job structure and social situation**
10:15	Break (coffee/tea)
10:30	Lecture on **Increasing productivity and creation of innovation capacity in SME's**
12:00	Lunch break
13:00	Group activity on increasing productivity and creation of innovation capacity in SME's
14:00	Lecture on **Tackling the consultation needs of women and elderly**
15:30	Company visits
17:30	End of the Day 1

Day 2 Programme

9:00	Group activity on consultation needs of women and elderly (including reflections from the company visits)
10:15	Break (coffee/tea)
10:30	Lecture on **Organizing effective consultations**
11.15	Discussion on learning from the best practices and the worst case
11:45	Evaluation of the Train the Consultant course
12:00	Lunch

5.6 Results of the training courses feedbacks

5.6.1 Train the Trainer 20/09/2012 Vilnius, Lithuania

Organizer was Lithuanian University of Educational Sciences.

Summary

Participants were asked to fill in the evaluation form in order to get valuable feedback about the course Train the Trainer. The results that were gained are presented shortly in this summary. First, participants were asked to present their satisfaction regarding the course. Participants were most pleased with the working atmosphere and the organization/support during the course. Participants would have wanted to have better ratio of theory and practice.

When participants were asked to rate the course, the best evaluations were gained from the section "the aims of the Train the Trainer course were clear". Participants rated also the sections "I was able to reflect the contents of the course with my previous experience" and "I learned knowledge and skills which will be necessary in the future" quite high. Improvements should be done with the participation, because the poorest evaluation was with the sections "I participated active in the discussion" and "I participate actively in the group activity".

Participants were asked to list strengths of the course. They were pleased with the combination of theory and practice, and the course material. In the section, where participants were asked to list the weaknesses, many participants wanted to have longer course and some did not find the clear objectives for the course. When participants were asked to suggest improvements of the course, they listed for example that the course should be longer and that the trainers should improve their action. In the beginning they would have also wanted to have a short introduction about the next step for trainees. Some would have wanted to have more course content suggested of how women and elderly could be empowered.

Trainees also listed important things or topics they learned during the course, and the most important one was innovation. They listed also things that they thought were missing. They would had wanted to have more discussion about what a training course should look like and what kind of specific issues consultants have to concentrate on in case of consulting managers. Participants would have also wanted to have an introduction on the consulting business if they needed to train the consultants.

Participants though that there was an appropriate amount of material covered during the course and that they will have the opportunity to utilize the training skills they have gained during the course within the coming months. Participants were told to list also when and how they would apply the skills gained from the course. Most of them said that during their own work and training sessions.

When participants were asked to rate the course in terms of usefulness, most of the participants though that the course was very useful/useful in their daily work. They also rated that the course would increase their willingness to train others. Less than half of the participants though that the course would increase their ability to train consultants.

The participants evaluated the group activities and they though there was enough time to complete the assignments, but not too much time was spend with the groups.

When the trainer was asked to evaluate, participants thought that the best appearance was when the trainer taught technically accurate content and when the trainer handled questions and comments with calm courtesy. Participants evaluated the trainer poorest in involving the audience.

The comments regarding the whole Train the Trainer course included requests to provide participants contact list with e-mail addresses and to provide a certificate for attendance of seminar and thus giving some certain rights to train others.

5.6.2   Train the Trainer 13/09/2013 Bialystok, Poland

Organizer was Białystok Foundation of Professional Training.

Summary

Participants were asked to fill in the evaluation form in order to get valuable feedback about the course Train the Trainer. The evaluation form was translated into Polish, and the results were translated back into English. The evaluation was comprehensive, and almost all parts of the proposed evaluation form were in use. The results (14 responses) that were gained are presented shortly in this summary. First, participants were asked to present their satisfaction regarding the course. Participants were satisfied or very satisfied with the whole course: ration of theory and practice, structure of the programme, pace at lectures, schedule of the course day, linking previous knowledge and practices, course materials, organization support and working atmosphere.

When participants were asked to rate the course, all evaluation criteria got at least good remarks. The dispersion between good, very good and excellent was roughly quite similar in most of the criteria: 10 %, 60 % and 30 %. Participants' rating in the sections "The aims of the Train the Trainer course were clear", "I participated active in the discussion" and "I participate actively in the group activity" dispersed slightly more, i.e. 15 % good, 50 % very good and 35 % excellent in the first one, and 30 % good, 35 % very good and 35 % excellent in the last two ones.

When participants were asked to rate the course in terms of usefulness, most of the participants (only one give rating somewhat useful) though that the course was useful or very useful in their daily work. They also rated that the course would increase their willingness to train others.

The evaluation question on women attitudes raised more scattered ratings. Especially in evaluation points "Entrepreneurs appreciate women's potential at the workplace" and "In BSR countries there are still present the stereotypes on women in the workplace" the answers scattered quite much. In the first one 15 % tend to disagree, and 85 % tend to agree or strongly agreed on the statement. In the latter one 7 % tend to disagree, 23 % neither agreed nor disagreed, and 70 % agreed or strongly agreed. 93 % agreed or strongly agreed that the way to increase professional activity of women is to promote their entrepreneurship, including setting up new firms. All respondent agreed or strongly agreed the statement that flexible forms of employment will in-crease the participation of women in the labor market. In 78 % of the respondent's organizations the solutions to help women to combine their professional duties and family responsibilities are applied. Examples of these solutions were flexible working hours, possibility of working at home, and company's kindergarten.

The ratings to the statements related to elderly attitudes were interesting. 77 % agreed or strongly agreed that the Baltic Sea Region countries are still not prepared for the economic consequences of the process of population ageing. 57 % said that Entrepreneurs are aware of demographic changes, and 23 % tend to disagree. 43 % disagreed or strongly disagreed that entrepreneurs do appreciate the potential of workers aged 50 +, while 36 % agreed or strongly agreed on that. Flexible forms of employment will increase the participation of older persons in the labor market in 64 % of the responses. Similarly 64 % said that the way to increase professional activity of the elderly is to promote entrepreneurship among this age group, and employees 55+ with much experience and knowledge, do not have skills to transmit their knowledge to younger workers. The latter got 23 % responses where the statement was disagreed or strongly disagreed. In 71 % of the answers the respondents said that in BSR countries there are still present the stereotypes on older people in the workplace. However, in 42 % there are no stereotypes related to older people in their own workplace.

Participants were asked to list strengths of the course. They were pleased with interesting issues, applicable examples, exercises and group works during the training, and discussions and direct contact with the speaker. The highlights of the course were the active participation of the attendants, good contact between the speakers and the participants, clear and understandable explanations of CSR issues. The participants emphasized that raising awareness among entrepreneurs of the importance of relations between employees and good atmosphere in the working place is a thing of utmost importance.

In the section, where participants were asked to list the weaknesses, the participants complained about too small texts and figures in the presentation slides and training materials. The time reserved for discussions was too short, and the topics could only be skimmed cursorily.

When participants were asked to suggest improvements of the course, they wanted to put more emphasis on small enterprises.

Trainers also listed important things or topics they learned during the course. They raised up CSR in an enterprise, stakeholders diagnosis and seeking, and that good relations with stakeholders bring only profits to the company, importance and ways of conducting social dialogue, necessity to overcome stereotypes, noticing women's strengths and potential in business, taking care of employees and good social relations are the foundation for proper functioning of an enterprise, and possibility of implementing new strategies to develop the company and to make it perceived as a reliable and good employer.

5.6.3   Train the Consultant, 26/10/2012 Brest, Belarus

Summary

For the evaluation of training, the organizer 'Lithuanian University of Educational

Sciences' had prepared only a comprehensive questionnaire in English. Because not all participants from Belarus spoke English, was the questionnaire translated and replied with the help of interpreters. This was very time consuming, caused confusion and finally had to be canceled. Only a few participants could at least partially fill in the answer sheet and submit.

Failing was therefore at the end of training an open discussion with questions below.

-Did the training fully fill your expectations of the participation of the training?

-Would you recommend the training to your friends?

-What was especially good at the training?

-What was rather poor and should be improved in future training?

The answers of the participants can be summarized as follows:

- "I came with modest expectations. Now I've a half book full of notes with important information".
- "I can just support this idea, for example: winning elderly for a profession, work with young people who are passive, to encourage them. We are ready and will join the project".
- "Representative of a Science Centre: the findings to gain social power in companies were especially good and valuable for me".

- "We work mostly with young people. Especially valuable is the knowledge that the mix of teams is crucial for me: younger and elder - women and men".
- "I am very grateful for the training, it has taken me further".
- "My expectations were fulfilled 100 %. It is a pity that there was so little time for the exchange of views".
- "I did learn a lot, I will implement 80 %".
- My expectations were more than fulfilled".
- "For me particularly positive is, that I realized, there are big differences, but also much common ground between countries and together we can solve the problems".
- "I received many concrete instructions for options, how I can make my future work better".
- "It was a very active group with a huge desire for discussions and questions".
- I get much valuable information".
- The frame, rooms, coffee, drinks, etc. were very good".
- "Perfect organization and good preparation".
- Lunch with plenty of time was also very positive".
- "There was nothing wrong, I am very happy".
- "Very positive for me were many concrete examples of promotions and mediation of international examples and experiences."

10 participants equal said: valuable training. We want continue to work on the topic, and necessarily participate in the elaboration of a strategic programme for Belarus.

5.6.4 Train the Consultant 07/03 – 08/03/2013 Gdansk, Poland

Evaluation material from the workshop "How to encourage entrepreneurs to hire women and the elderly?"

Organizer: Faculty of Management and Economics, Gdansk University of Technology

Summary

Participants were asked to evaluate the importance of workshop topics. The evaluation scale was from 1(disagree) to 5 (agree) and the answers presented in this summary are based on the average values from the participants. The poorest average values in evaluation were gained from the sections:

- "Entrepreneurs do appreciate the potential of workers aged 50 +",
- "Entrepreneurs appreciate women's potential at the workplace",
- "Employees 55+ with much experience and knowledge, do not have skills to transmit their knowledge to younger workers",
- "In my organization there are still present the stereotypes on older people in the workplace", and
- "In my organization there are still present the stereotypes on women in the workplace".

To the last section participants were asked to write examples and one of the participants gave an example: "Woman is a mother (1st role), who avoid additional tasks. She isn't disposable".

The highest average values in evaluation were gained from the sections:

- "Flexible forms of employment will increase the participation of women in the labour market",
- "Mentoring is the key action for the preservation of organizational knowledge",
- "Staff team in my organization is age -diverse", and
- "In my organization, the tasks are performed by intergenerational teams".

Participants were asked to give examples to few sections. To the section "In my organization there are still present the stereotypes on older people in the workplace" participants gave examples such as: "Older people are poorly oriented in the current situation", and "Elders are less effective, avoid of involvement, are refractory of new technologies". To the section "In my organization there are applied solutions to help women to combine their professional duties and family responsibilities" participants gave examples such as: "Women can work less (i.e. part-time) when their children are young or ill. Men has the same right in Finland", and "We have flexible forms of employment".

Participants evaluated also the workshop assessment and high values were gained from all the participants to all sections. Participants unanimously agreed that "Trainers were well prepared for classes", "Workshop motivated and involved participants", "I intend to use knowledge from the workshop at work", and "Workshop was well-organized".

General comments about the workshop are presented below.

- "The workshop was really interesting and rewarding."
- "Good selection of topics of workshop, especially psychological issues, which have a big influence in the recruitment of elders or women."
- "Preparation and conduction of workshop was professional. It is a great need of talk about these issues according to the low employers' awareness in this field."

5.6.5   Train the Consultant 19/09 – 20/09/2013 Riga, Latvia

Evaluation material from the workshop "Innovative SMEs by Gender and Age"

Organizer: VISC, National Centre for Education

Summary:

Participants were asked to fill in the evaluation form in order to get valuable feed-back about the course Train the Consultant. The evaluation was comprehensive, and almost all parts of the proposed evaluation form were in use. The results (16 responses) that were gained are presented shortly in this summary. First, participants were asked to present their satisfaction regarding the course. All participants were satisfied or very satisfied with the whole course: ration of theory and practice, structure of the programme, schedule of the course day, linking previous knowledge and practices, course materials, organization support and working atmosphere. 12 participants were satisfied or very satisfied with the pace at lectures, and four neither satisfied nor dissatisfied.

When participants were asked to rate the course, the aims of the Train the Consultant course were clear, the methods of instruction were consistent with the learning outcomes and I learned knowledge and skills which will be necessary in my professional activities got at least good remarks. The questions on "the study facilities and equipment were appropriate for learning", "active participation in the discussions was encouraged" and "I participated actively in the group activity" were rated to be very good or excellent. The rating for the questions "I was able to reflect the content of Train the Consultant course with my previous experience" and "The training inspired me to study more of the subject" dispersed a lot, from excellent to average. However, ten participants rated these very good or excellent.

When participants were asked to rate the course in terms of usefulness, most of the participants though that the course was useful or very useful in their daily work. They also rated that the course would increase their willingness to consult and train others.

The evaluation question on women attitudes raised more scattered ratings. 31 % tend to disagree on the statement "Entrepreneurs appreciate women's potential at the workplace" and 19 % agreed, others neither disagreed nor agreed. 12 % tend to disagree, 12 % agreed, 12 % strongly agreed and others neither disagreed not agrees on the evaluation point "In BSR countries there are still present the stereotypes on women in the work-place".

62 % agreed or strongly agreed, and 12 % disagreed that the way to increase professional activity of women is to promote their entrepreneurship, including setting up new firms. All respondent, except one, agreed or strongly agreed the statement that flexible forms of employment will in-crease the participation of women in the labour market. In 62 % of the respondent's organizations the solutions to help women to combine their professional duties and family responsibilities are applied. Example of the solution was that women with small babies until the age of 18 month can finish their working day one hour before official working time.

The ratings to the statements related to elderly attitudes were interesting. 88 % agreed or strongly agreed that the Baltic Sea Region countries are still not prepared for the economic consequences of the process of population ageing. 69 % said that Entrepreneurs are aware of demographic changes. 49 % disagreed or strongly disagreed that entrepreneurs do appreciate the potential of workers aged 50 +, while

12 % agreed or strongly agreed on that. Flexible forms of employment will increase the participation of older persons in the labour market in 62 % of the responses. Half of the participants rated that the way to increase professional activity of the elderly is to promote entrepreneurship among this age group. 56 % said that employees 55+ with much experience and knowledge do not have skills to transmit their knowledge to younger workers. All answer options were in use in the statement "In BSR countries there are still present the stereotypes on older people in the workplace". Half of them said that they agree or strongly agree on the statement, and 25 % said that they tend to disagree or strongly disagree. The age of staff is diverse in 88 % of the participants work teams. However, in 38 % there are no stereotypes related to older people in their own workplace.

Participants gave free comments on the course as follows:

- "Great seminar to have both theoretical and practical things, many new ideas and suggestions how to improve female and elderly situation in BSR and Latvia. This was done in a perfect way".

- "During the seminar not only theoretical and factual knowledge was gained but also specific examples, which inspired to develop new innovations and deepened the understanding of what exactly is an innovation. Very good organization of the seminar and skilful work with the audience, also time management. A chance to meet and have a discussion with people from various fields. A feeling of support".

- "I might have wanted to hear some more examples of life experience not only statistical information. As I am a practical person and have achieved everything in life on my own. But it was truly great to meet different and smart people, who can teach me a lot!"

- "This seminar gave me a chance to "sit down", take a break from every day routine in work and share my thoughts, ideas and see myself from other perspective as well as see our country with more open eyes. This definitely enriches and pushes ourselves to innovations".

- "Interesting, globalized point of view on role and place of women and seniors currently and in the future. Definition of innovations (what is the content of innovations). Interesting discussions. A chance to visit a small enterprise. Work in groups, proposals for successful entrepreneurship. Interesting, active and very attractive event".

- "The promoted topic in the Project „QUICK IGA" is currently very important and should be operatively realized in government institutions. The developed Memorandum of Understanding is remarkable, but there should be mentioned also solutions for the problems in practice not only theoretical support. I am grateful for smoothly organized event, which offered statistical information and a chance to establish valuable contacts for future cooperation with other participants. Also thank you for creative ideas, how to give my own support for problem solutions."

- Benefits of the seminar: "New information on demographic situation and activities of Project Quick IGA.; A chance to meet with experts of various fields; A chance to have a discussion with colleagues; Inspiration to develop innovations in my own work place".

- "I am very happy with the practical approaches to innovations".

5.6.6 Conclusions

Two Train the Trainer- courses and three Train the Consultant- courses were organized. The evaluation of these was made by distributing the participants the feedback forms to fill in. The participants were overall pleased with the training sessions and they gave good feedback.

The duration of the training courses was:

- Train the Trainer 1 day
- Train the Consultants 1 - 2 days

This feedback report was based on the following training sessions:

- Train the Trainer
    - 20.9.2012 Vilnius, Lithuania
    - 13.9.2013 Bialystok, Poland

- Train the Consultant

    - 26.10.2012 Brest, Belarus
    - - 8.3.2013 Gdansk, Poland
    - 19. - 20.09.2013 Riga, Latvia

In order to improve the feedback system, it would be important to get some constructive feedback and not only positive evaluation about everything. Specific questions about the fails and faults could be useful. The feedback form should be translated to the participants own language. This could improve the evaluation and rating of the courses.

In the future Train the Trainer courses will be transferred to 15 Universities from 9 BSR countries (Member of Baltic Sea Academy). The Train the Consultant course will be transferred to 50 Chambers from 11 BSR countries (Members of Hanseatic Parliament).

For further information, see: University of Satakunta and University of Vilnius.

6. Instruments for the management of demographic change at the enterprise

6.1. Introduction

The demographic change will affect all the countries in the Baltic Sea region but with specific manifestations in each case. The degree and the type of challenges are described in detail in numerous publications. Many (especially larger) enterprises prepare for two fundamental challenges,

- to find solutions for the growing share of older employees and at the same time
- to be attractive for young professionals.

For the gainful employment which should be performed until the (increasing) retirement age there is a requirement to organize working conditions so that as many people as possible could, wanted and were allowed to work in well-being, healthily, gladly and productively until their retirement.

Age- and ageing-appropriate work should consider personal capacities and individual needs as well as changes of working requirements. These factors change over the course of the professional life. The task of the enterprises and the employees is therefore to adapt them in line with demand and in due time so that the working capacity could be retained and the productivity was guaranteed.

Therefore it is necessary to bring into focus the possibilities for the management of the demographic change for the enterprises. In this case two basic approaches can become effective.

- **Ensuring professional future which will be robust with respect to demography**
  Enterprises and organizations must have the competence to be able to organize the future of their personnel and for their personnel actively and purposefully. The pre-condition thereto is careful personnel policy through the promotion of age- /ageing-appropriate and healthy working conditions.

- **Promotion** of the ability to perform the work
  The work must be able to be performed; as a rule it should be executable without health damage until the achievement of the retirement age. The working requirements and the individual capabilities therefore must correspond to the extent possible.

As the fields of action for age- and ageing-appropriate works all the professional and personal fields for the creation of beneficial working and living conditions should be mentioned: health, qualification/competence, corporate culture, leadership and motivation, and more specifically working conditions, i.e. working time, working environment, organization of work, ergonomics etc. as well as the right balance between work and private sphere.

This big range of fields of action scares many actors away. Often enterprises try to address separate topics hoping that it could already function somehow. For example, the ergonomics is being improved in order to reduce workload, behavior-oriented health trainings are offered to the employees or advertising campaigns are started for the trainees. These are good and important measures but as a rule they are not sufficient for the development of a predictive active strategy. For this purpose actually a more comprehensive approach is required which will consider not only separate aspects but also regard the overlaps between the professional areas of work. A pro-active strategy which describes the vision for the preservation/promotion of working ability and observes the whole professional life-course is sophisticated but surely more goal-oriented than not coordinated separate measures.

Such an approach considers all the possibilities for the influence on good (feasible, motivating, health-promoting, personality-promoting…) work during the whole working life-course, i.e. from entering the occupation to transition to the retirement.

Example:

Our male and female employees are the most important resource at the enterprise. We want to preserve and expand their capabilities and potentials by supporting and promoting all the employees in their working ability. Therefore the work must be adapted to the people.

We want to organize the conditions so that younger employees could adapt well to the activity and to the enterprise, we could offer good development chances to everybody and older persons could perform their work healthily, in a motivated manner and productively. The transition to the time after the employment phase is prepared in due time.

The following description of fields of action gives a corresponding overview. The representation of instruments does not claim the integrity.

6.2 Principal fields of action

The principal fields of action are:

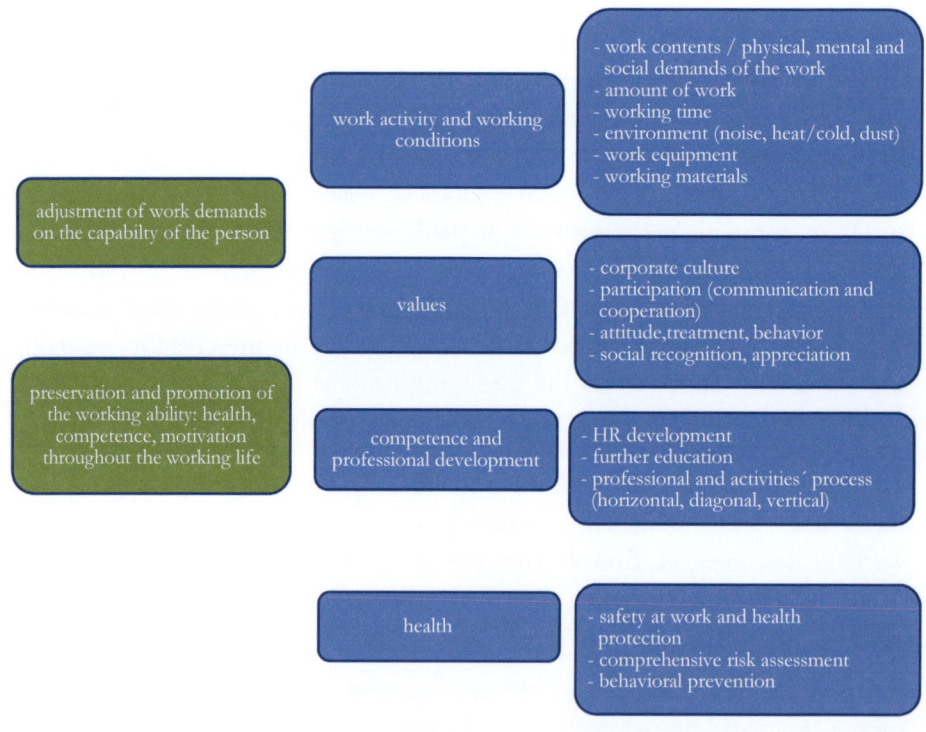

Diagram 1: fields of action for the promotion of employability in the demographic change

The **tasks for the work design** are as follows:

Appropriate organization of working activities for all age groups

- Organization of latitudes for activity
- Transfer of planned/arranged activities
- Securing contentual flexibility
- Social integration

Introduction of more flexible working time structures

- More often, individually usable short breaks
- Reduction of working hours
- More flexible retirement programs
- Part-time working relations

Avoiding critical working conditions for older employees

- Work under time pressure
- Demand to high speed of movement, high requirements to the capacity of reaction and attention
- High adaptation requirements to visual perception

Considering factors of influence on performance resources

- Private lifestyle
- Education, socialization
- Previous activities (workloads, training)
- Performance incentives
- Learning incentives
- Promoting working conditions

The most important aspects in the fields of action taking into account age-/ageing-critical working requirements as well as references to possibilities of organization are assembled further in the form of examples.

Work organization, work design and working time

- Working requirements and performance capability, first of all in case of physically demanding works
- Lifting and carrying loads, forced postures, unilaterally straining activities,
- Working atmosphere burdens
  - Noise, climate (heat, coldness), dust/dirt, lighting, vibration
- Work equipment (ergonomics)
- Working materials, first of all dangerous materials
- Amount of working time or rigid performance specifications
  - Cycle-related work, activities with short cycle, time pressure
  - Shift and night work
- Working rhythm not in compliance with the "biological clock", social disadvantages
  - High physical loads (see below)
- Sustained attention, stress, frequent disturbances/interruptions

High level of physical stress at the working place

- Employees often work at the limit of their performance ability
- The deadline and responsibility pressure increases
- Problems with colleagues and superiors right up to mobbing become more frequent
- Conflicts occur with (external or internal) customers
- Small faults by processing can have very far-reaching consequences
- There is not enough time for the exchange with colleagues
- There is more work overtime or employees work during breaks

Age and autonomy at the working place

- Organization of breaks
- Order of working tasks
- Diversion of working methods
- Diversion of working speed
- Load change
- Avoiding over-/underload
- Application according to changed competence

Possibilities of the employees for the health-preserving work

- Health-preserving lifting, carrying, grasping
- Use of technical aids
- Mutual help and support
- Change of load and variety by introduction of various activities and rotation
- Use of body protection
- Reasonable interruptions and organization of breaks
- Relaxation techniques at the working place
- Corporate schemes for the promotion of health
- Development and submission of proposals for ergonomic improvements
- Possibilities for complaints due to working conditions which are critical for health

Organization of the working activity – reduction of time pressure

- Time pressure for older employees can lead to extreme physical and psychic loads due to strict deadlines and short terms
- High working tempo
- Safeguarding provisions for older employees make slower work possible through reduced planned performance or deadlines which are stipulated in tariff/employment agreements or work/service agreements.
- Underperformance of separate employees within the framework of the group work
- Often there is psychic pressure caused by time pressure based on orientations and standards of the employees themselves, not on working deadlines:
- Due to their habit to correspond to the image of a "good employee" employees put themselves under stress

Organization of working activity – health-preserving workmanship

- Here: *desk work*
  - Work taking care of the back
  - Hold the back section loosely and straight
  - Change the seated position all the time
  - Stand up and move from time to time

- If necessary use the standing desk/height-adjustable table

Distribution of responsibilities and group work

- Various performance capabilities during the allocation of tasks must be taken into account.
- Older persons do not get excessive demands; they can cope with their tasks in the team well.
- The compilation of tasks, professional qualification, wage and performance regulation and promotion of social competence are important.
- Differential allocation of tasks, performance differences are considered and individually passing solutions must be found.
- Social cohesion of the group must be promoted purposefully so that the weaker points of the older employees could be compensated by the group.

Age(ageing)-appropriate further training/knowledge and experience management

- Passing experience-based knowledge (contacts, organizational knowledge etc.)
- Letting younger professionals adapt smoothly
- By personnel reduction ensuring desirable knowledge, e.g. expert pools
- Mentoring
- Appreciation of the status of professional careers (horizontal careers) besides management careers; promotion of capability to change and learn through shift between tasks and positions.
- Promotion of lifelong competence development (e.g. activate middle-aged and elderly employees through change of activity and further training)
- Establishing balanced personnel and age structures in specific areas of work and throughout the company in order to avoid waves of recruitments and retirements.

Career management

- Transferring older employees from especially stressful fields of action to new positions at the enterprise according to their performance capability
- Constant position assignment by career management

- Load-oriented and individual-related planning of careers with qualification measures is important
- Individual conversation between employees (if desired together with BR) and management on a regular basis (e.g. within the framework of the annual discussion of objectives or approvals)
- Questions about interest in development prospects of the employee
- Suggestion of the corporate career paths for the employee(s)
- Determining the need for qualification/further training and times for the collection of expertise in the particular field
- Agreement of the transfer of knowledge to younger professionals
- Agreement of the term for determination

Organization of working time

- Unloading older employees by changing the position, duration and distribution of the working time
- The duration of the load effect can be reduced by using measures of reduction of the working time
- Position, duration and distribution of the working time shall be organized so that older employees could "economize"

Possibilities for the reduction of working hours

- by activities with high pressure it must lead to noticeable unloading
- smooth transition to the retirement and partial retirement
- instead of block model smooth transition: working life model
- only successfully without work intensification in the remaining time

Project management

A comprehensive and strategic demography management as a rule requires project-shaped development which develops a comprehensive plan,

- ➢ why anything
- ➢ where/at what position
- ➢ with what objective
- ➢ how

> - from whom
> - till when it must be done
> - and how the control of effect and if necessary the change will be implemented.

Without elevating the efforts: it can be done also at small and medium-sized enterprises systematically and best of all with the participation of the employees.

6.3 Instruments for the management of demographic change and of intervention

Further several references, counseling tools, strategic recommendations and qualification offers are presented which can support the enterprises to implement a (more) scheduled demographic policy.

They are different with regard to instruments/references which take place with external support (Chapter 1: Counseling tools) and in activities/measures which can be implemented by the enterprise on its own (Chapter 2).

6.3.1 Instruments for consultation

1.	Work Ability Index = Analysis of the individual stress
2.	Work accomplishment coaching®
2.a	Qualifying workshop for the utilization of the counseling tool "Work accomplishment coaching®"
3.	Personnel management with stable demography Structural analysis according to age, gender, competence profile etc. for the simulation of the personnel requirement (HC-Score)

1. Measuring the work accomplishment ability with the Work Ability Index

Work Ability describes the potential of a person to accomplish the requirement to the indicated point in time.

Thereby individual functional (physical, spiritual, psychic and social) capacities are regarded with respect to the work requirement.

Both items – work and person – can change with time passing and if necessary they must be organized in the age-/ageing- and health-appropriate manner.

Extensive research of the Finish Institute of Occupational Health on the work ability of older workers has identified the core factors affecting work ability. The research findings can be depicted in the form of a 'work ability house' with four floors.

The three lower floors of the house describe the individual resources: (1) health and functional capacities, (2) competence, (3) values, attitudes and motivation. The fourth floor covers working life. Staircases between the floors indicate that all floors of the house are interacting. Besides the workplace, also family and close community influence the balance.

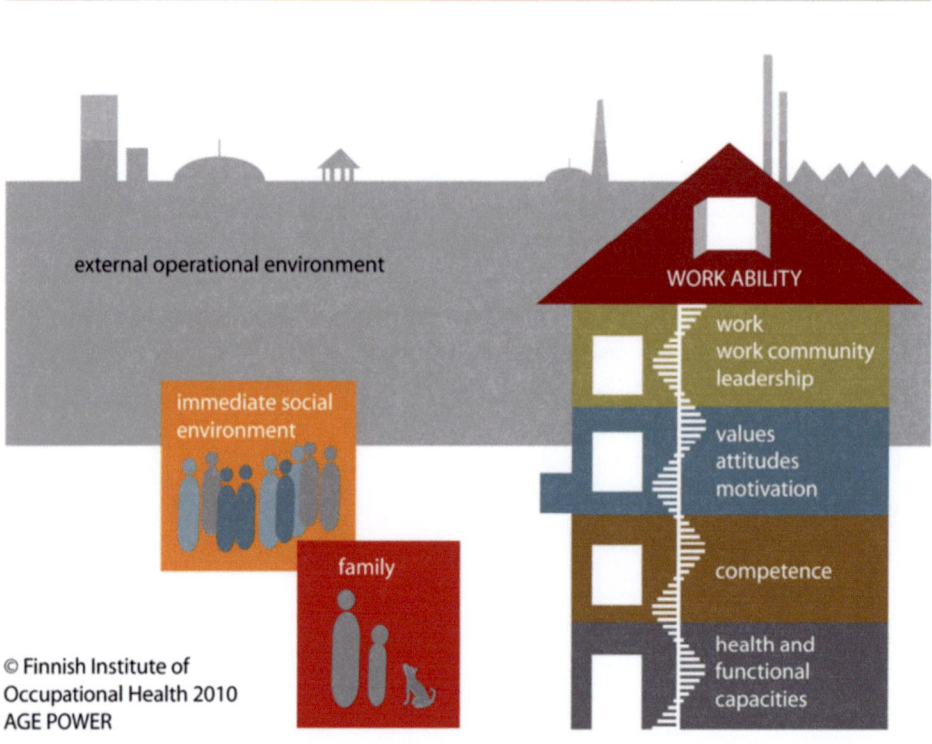

Diagram 2: The "House of work capabilty"

Since both the work in terms of their requirements (technology, organisation, working hours, etc.) as well as the person (age, health, competence) may change over time, it is necessary to preserve the stability of work ability for the duration of the working life. This cannot be made by someone on their own – persons and businesses must work together so that the house could remain stable. This always requires appropriate maintenance and modernisation works.

In the corporate use, the concept of the house of work ability is directly instructive for action, when on each level the desired and the actual situation is systematically observed and the coordinated measures for the promotion of work ability can be implemented. This can be done in participatory processes at the working level, in circles or work in joint working groups for managers, work councils, as well as experts for personnel development, job design, occupational health and safety etc.

Work Ability can be measured. The Work Ability Index (WAI) is an internationally used survey instrument for the assessment of the current balance (stability and matching) between the work requirements and the personal capacities of a person. This is the instrument for the subjective stress analysis.

The WAI has been developed since 1980 at the Finnish Institute of Occupational Health (FIOH). Meanwhile it is translated in 28 languages.

The WAI contains the following 7 topics:

1. Current work accomplishment ability in comparison to the best one which was once achieved

2. Current work accomplishment in comparison to physical and spiritual requirements of the work

3. Number of current illnesses which have been diagnosed by the doctor

4. Assessed negative impact by work as a result of these illnesses

5. Sick leaves during the last 12 months

6. Own forecast of the work accomplishment ability from now on for the following two years

7. Psychic/mental resources and states

The index number lies between 7 and 49 points; the higher the point value is, the more distinct is the work accomplishment ability.

For the better handling and as the support of interpretation of results the distinction between four work accomplishment constellations is made which are related to specific protection and promotion goals:

Number of WAI points	WA constellation	Protection and promotion objective
44 – 49	1. Very good	Preserve work accomplishment
37 – 43	2. Good	Support work accomplishment
28 – 36	3. Moderate	Improve work accomplishment
07 – 27	4. Critical	Restore work accomplishment

The WAI is implemented in Finland as a standard instrument during first and repeated occupational health checks, e.g. by the Occupational Health Service.

Also in Germany the WAI is frequently used as an instrument within the framework of the occupational and medical anamnesis.

The WAI is expressively used by preventive consultants who are committed to confidentiality. It is not the instrument for appraisal interviews which are held by the management. The use by other persons (groups) requires special agreement or data protection and confidentiality.

The WAI is a simple method which can be personally passed online (see, for example, http://www.arbeitsfaehigkeit.uni-wuppertal.de/index.php?WAI-Online), but as a rule it is used as the questionnaire in the institutional procedure during which it must be filled in by the person independently.

Within the framework of the risk assessment the WAI requires the supplement by the condition-related work analysis (loads and organization resources). In the participative organizational and personal development process Work Accomplishment Coaching (➔ see Chapter 1.2) the WAI is integrated in the counseling process.

In several European countries (e.g. Germany, Austria, the Netherlands, Luxemburg) there is a WAI network.

References to the **Reliability** of the instruments can be found in

- *Ilmarinen, Juhani (2007):* The Work Ability Index (WAI), in: Occupational Medicine 2007; 57:160
- *Zwart B.; Frings-Dresen M. (2002):* Test-retest reliability of the Work Ability Index questionnaire. Occupational Medicine; 52: 177–181.

Literature

- *Ilmarinen, Juhani (2005):* Towards a Longer Worklife! Ageing and the quality of worklife in the European Union, Finnish Institute of Occupational Health / Ministry of Social Affairs and Health. Helsinki .
- *Nygård C-H. ; Savinainen M.; Tapio K.; Lumme-Sandt K. (eds.) (2011):* Age Management during the Life Course. Proceedings of the 4th Symposium on Work Ability. Tampere.
- *Tuomi, Kaija; Ilmarinen, Juhani; Jahkola, Antti; Katajarinne, Lea; Tulkki, Arto (1982):* Work Ability Index. Finnish Institute of Occoupational Health. Helsinki.
  [in german:] *Hasselhorn, Hans Martin & Freude, Gabriele (2007):* Der Work Ability Index – ein Leitfaden. Schriftenreihe der Bundesanstalt für Arbeitsschutz und Arbeitsmedizin, Sonderschrift S 87. Dortmund / Berlin / Dresden.

2. Work accomplishment coaching®

An age- and ageing-appropriate work should take into account personal capacities and individual needs as well as work requirements. These factors change during the professional life. The task of the enterprises and the employees is therefore to adapt them in line with the demand in good time in order to preserve health and to ensure productivity.

The degree of matching work and person can be obtained with the help of the Work Ability Index. Using the counseling tool "Work accomplishment coaching" in connection with the assessment of the current situation by means of the Work Ability Index (WAI → see Chapter 1.1) with each employee at the enterprise individual promotion resolutions and corporate promotion measures for the accomplishment of work requirements are developed. The results of all the interviews serve to the corporate decision-makers for the planning and implementation of advantageous working conditions.

The consultation process with the work accomplishment coaching®

The work accomplishment coaching is a two-stage development process (see figure 1). The significant modules of the consultation process are illustrated in the graphic.

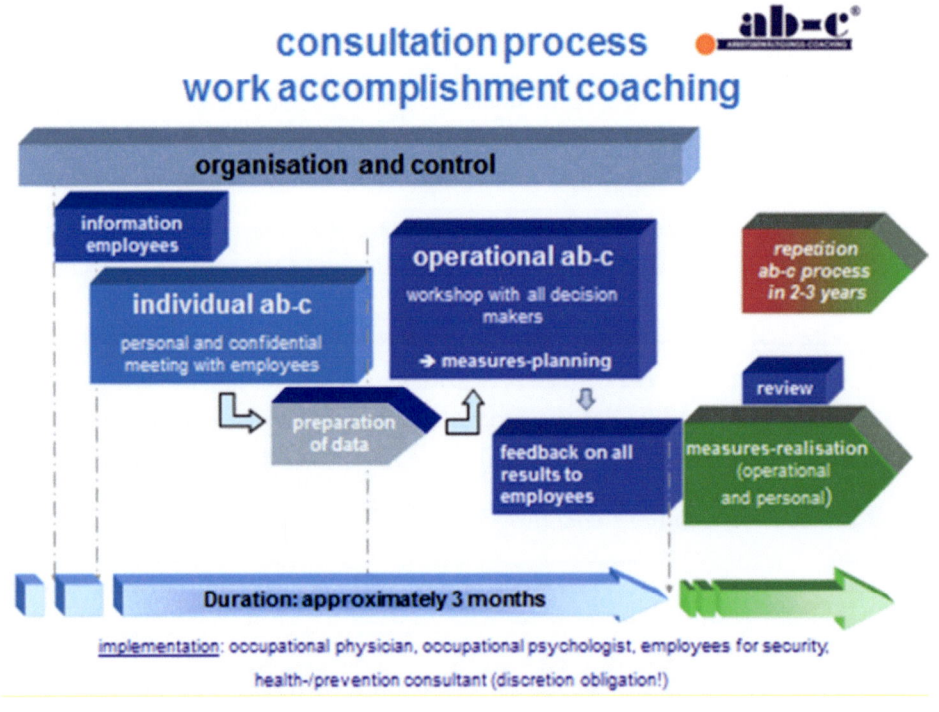

Diagram 3: The consultation process for the work accomplishment coaching

For the use at the enterprise first of all they must be necessarily agreed with the management, workforce representatives and specialists from the fields of occupational safety and medicine (project management circle). Among other things the orientation of the goal at the implementation of measures, type and scope of the information about employees, timing and regulations for data protection must be agreed.

The ab-c interview

The personal and confidential ab-c is the offer for all the employees at the enterprise. The participation at the interview which lasts about one hour is voluntary.

First of all the current work accomplishment situation is studied with the help of the Work Ability Index and the result is explained to the discussion partner. Further the discussion partners are guided with the use of questions to search for personal as well as corporate measures for the promotion (preservation, support, improvement or restoration) of the work accomplishment and to think about the implementation steps. The fundamental questions are the following:

- What can you do to promote your work accomplishment ability?

- What do you need from the enterprise?

Both questions are asked in the four crucial areas of design: health, competence, working conditions, management/work organization. For the individual promotion resolutions each person concludes an agreement with himself: "I want to do this. I will begin so". An individual and demand-oriented promotion plan for the achievement of the own promotion and protection goal is created.

The goal of the ab-c interview is self-observation (where I stay), self-regulation (what I can/want to do myself) and also the development of suggestions for corporate measures for the preservation and promotion of the work accomplishment ability.

Examples:

- Intensification of sports – start with fitness and Nordic walking in the morning.
- Wish me stress management training; the enterprise should support the course taking (working time).
- Huge time pressure – quality may not suffer; early coordination with other processors and between the masters is required.

- Earlier planning would be better for thinking for oneself; arrangement of monthly planning discussions of management with team spokesmen.
- People must be more motivated e.g. through recognition of the performed work.
- Further training planning in the beginning of the year would be good.

All the promotion intentions and references are recorded in the minutes. The employees receive copies of their work accomplishment situation and of their promotion plan.

Absolute confidentiality by handling personal data and contents is the essential basic precondition for the success of the interview and for the positive effect among the participants.

Evaluation and work accomplishment report

Including several structural data the work accomplishment report is created. The work ability situation of the staff is aggregated. The promotion intentions and suggestions from the ab-c interview are registered anonymously and prepared so that nobody is identifiable. With the help of the catchword index a simple count of frequency of topics is possible.

Corporate work accomplishment workshop

The results of the survey are presented to the steering committee of the enterprise at the ab-c workshop. The goal is to formulate corporate promotional measures on the basis of findings about the work ability of the staff and the corresponding promotional needs. The central questions are:

- What can the enterprise do to promote the work accomplishment ability of the staff?
- What does the enterprise need from outside?

The expected result of the workshop is the agreement of at least one promotional measure – ideally at all four levels of activity: health promotion, working conditions, personal development and career planning, management and work organization.

At the corporate ab-c on the basis of references of the employees the measures for the organization of work and for the promotion of work accomplishment ability are derived, they are assessed according to their importance (important/urgent) and transferred to the corporate development projects (planning of expenditures and resources).

Possible applications and benefits of the work accomplishment coaching

The ab-c crosses the levels of the person and the enterprise. Everybody takes part in the preventive and stabilizing arrangement of the house of work ability. Persons and organizations are encourages to become active and to act creatively. The process consulting encourages the development of individual solutions and accompanies the people without taking away the decision and the responsibility from them.

The benefits of the enterprise are describable:

- Work ability becomes a practicable basis of control for the predictive and sustainable personnel management.
- The work ability of the staff becomes plannable and shapeable.
- Personal policy based on the ab-c strengthens the employee loyalty and creates attractive, employee-oriented working conditions.

During the consulting process the employees get the opportunity

- for the planning and organization of their life and work quality,
- for the adaptation of working conditions according to the needs as the basis for health preservation and the increase of well-being at work,
- for the working life which will endanger the enjoyment of the third chapter in life to the least possible extent.

The work accomplishment coaching®

- determines important impulses at work,
- shows the state and the development potentials of work accomplishment of the personnel,
- contributes t the corporate dialogue for the good work,

- ensures the participation of employees in the planning and implementation of optimization measures and
- is therefore effective as a preventive and curative measure.

For the utilization of the ab-c the basic condition is that the enterprise and the employee had the passion and the courage to get involved in an open and unbiased process. All the experiences show that strong and the points are identified to a large extent and practicable references are developed for the individual and corporate organization of good and beneficial working conditions.

The work accomplishment coaching® may be usable in all branches and is well suitable for small and medium-sized enterprises. The process consulting is performed by trained consultants (→ for the qualification see Chapter 1.2.a). The goal of the application is to support employees and enterprises in their self-observation and self-management competence and also to implement measures for the organization/change not only at the individual but also at the corporate level.

Literature

- *Arbeit und Zukunft e.V. (Hrsg.)(2006):* Dialoge verändern. Partizipative Arbeitsgestaltung – Voraussetzungen, Methoden und Erfahrungen für eine zukunftsfähige Arbeitsforschung. Köln

- *Bundesanstalt für Arbeitsschutz- und Arbeitsmedizin / Initiative Neue Qualität der Arbeit (Hrsg.) / Wissenschaftliche Ausarbeitung: Brigitta Gruber und Alexander Frevel (2013):* Das Individuum stärken, die betriebliche Zukunft sichern. Arbeitsbewältigungs-Coaching® als Antwort auf neue Herausforderungen. 2. aktualisierte Auflage, Dortmund/Berlin.

- *INQA – Initiative Neue Qualität der Arbeit: Arbeitsbewältigungs-Coaching - Der Leitfaden zur Anwendung im Betrieb [Text: Brigitta Gruber, Alexander Frevel] (2012).* INQA-Bericht 38, Berlin (2. überarb. Aufl.).

- *Gruber, Brigitta / Frevel, Alexander / Vogel, Kaspar:* Work Ability Coaching – a new tool encouraging individuals, businesses and industries to handle the demographic change process, in: Clas-Håkan Nygård/Minna

Savinainen/Tapio Kirsi/Kirsi Lumme-Sandt (eds.) (2011): Age Management during the Life Course. Proceedings of the 4th Symposium on Work Ability. Tampere.

Tempel, Jürgen / Ilmarinen, Juhani: Arbeitsleben 2025. Das Haus der Arbeitsfähigkeit im Unternehmen bauen. Hrsg. von Marianne Giesert, Hamburg 2013

2.a Guidelines and qualification seminar for the application of the counseling tool "Work accomplishment coaching®"

The application of the counseling tool "Work accomplishment coaching®" requires basically

- the completion of a working or health science studies (e.g. occupational medicine, occupational psychology, ergonomics, health management or the like)
- and also the experience in the counseling of enterprises/organizations.

On this basis and after the self-experience of a personal work accomplishment interview employees can take part in the two-days qualifying workshop. With the completion the process can be performed according to the published guidelines[12] and the word/image logo can be used.

Every year about six open and if necessary additional in-house workshops are held in Germany and Austria. See: www.arbeitsbewaeltigungscoaching.net

Educational contents

- Age(-ing)-appropriate work
- The tool: work accomplishment coaching®
    - personal and confidential interview
    - corporate workshop – how enterprises come to doing it

---

[12] Federal Agency for Industrial Health and Safety / Initiative New Quality of Work (ed.) / Text: Brigitta Gruber and Alexander Frevel: Work accomplishment coaching. Guideline for the application at the enterprise. Report No. 38, 2. Revised edition, Dortmund/Berlin 2012

- inter-company starting points – activity groups, branches, regions
- Theoretical and practical fundamentals
  - Work Ability Index (WAI)[13]
  - Consulting components
  - Input and evaluation of data
  - Representation of results
  - Implementation of measures
  - Attitude of the consultants
- Individual test of the personal and confidential interview
- Group work to prepare a corporate workshop

The participants receive the certificate of attendance.

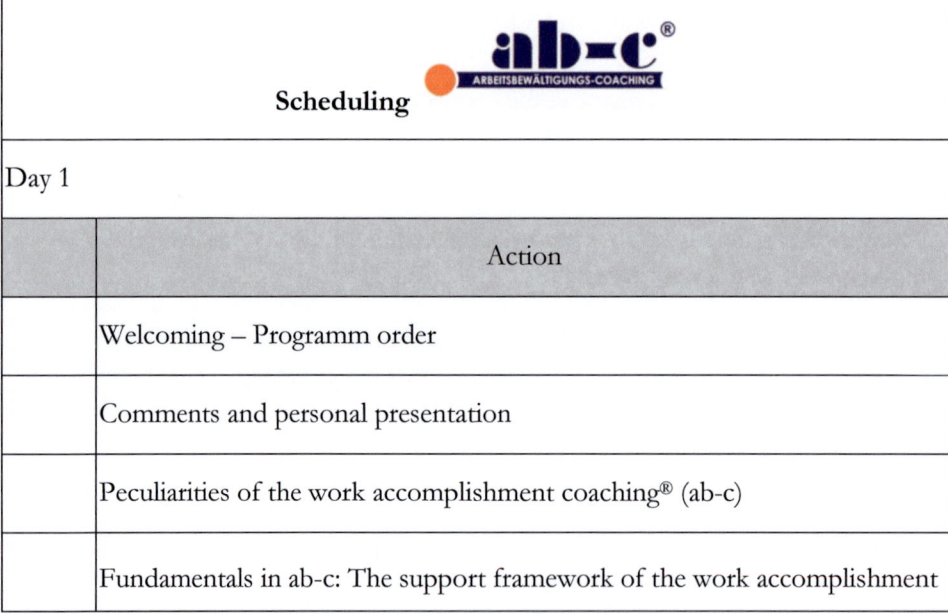

	ab-c® ARBEITSBEWÄLTIGUNGS-COACHING **Scheduling**	
Day 1		
	Action	
	Welcoming – Programm order	
	Comments and personal presentation	
	Peculiarities of the work accomplishment coaching® (ab-c)	
	Fundamentals in ab-c: The support framework of the work accomplishment	

---

[13] Tuomi, Kaija / Ilmarinen, Juhani / Jahkola, Antti / Katajarinne, Lea / Tulkki, Arto: Arbeitsbewältigungsindex. Work Ability Index. Series of the Federal Agency for Industrial Health and Safety, Translation Ü14, Dortmund/ Berlin 2001
Hasselhorn, Hans Martin / Freude, Gabriele: The Work Ability Index – guideline. Series of the Federal Agency for Industrial Health and Safety, Special report S 87, Dortmund/Berlin/Dresden 2007

	ability and the measuring/visualization instrument of the work ability index (WAI)
	Central component 1: personal and confidential ab-c
	Individual testing of the ab-c counseling techniques (pair groups)
Day 2	
	Action
	Reflection oft he self-test
	Central component 2: Corporate ab-c: feedback and measures planning
	Organization block A: Evaluation of discussions, (online) analysis tools and ab-c report
	Group exercise: Presentation and moderation concept "Corporate work accomplishment workshop"
	Central component 3 (optional): Regional/branch-related ab-c
	Organizational component B: Project start and project organization
	Quality assurance (ab-c laboratory); word-image logo: oral evaluation of the course and certificate of attendance

3. **Personnel management with stable demography**
   Structural analysis according to age, gender, competence profile for the
   simulation of personal needs
   (here: with the instrument HC-Score)

Often it helps when enterprises/organizations know the structure of their personnel at least according to age and if necessary according to further social and structural characteristics (gender, qualification, …) (→ see Chapter 2.1). The simple update for the following 5 or 10 years offers the first overview.

Among the marketable instruments there is one that stands out which is a little costlier in the data generation but thanks to the simulation capability it makes personal development more predictable.

HCscore[3] is a software solution for the analysis of dynamic effects of the demographic change in the personnel portfolio. It is more appropriate for enterprises with corresponding expertise and for demography consultants likewise.

The current staff of an enterprise is imported from the available table formats. In the system it is then possible to make an order according to enterprise-specific sorting structures such as e.g. branches, departments, professional groups, qualification levels, …).

Analysis

The staff can be examined with the help of the HCscore[3] for social and demographic key figures and factors (age, gender, nationality, …).
The graphics library allows comprehensive visualization using all usual chart types. All the tables and graphics are exportable and can be processed further.
With the help of the separate structure module differences between branches, locations, activity groups etc. can be put in relation with each other and can be analyzed comparatively.

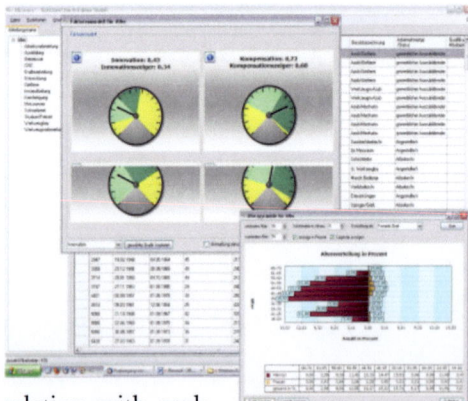

Simulation

Based on the current staff, taking into account such factors as fluctuation and planned increase or decrease of the number of personnel the future employee portfolio can be simulated. How does the enterprise grow old? Where are the bottlenecks?

Various scenarios are possible for the whole enterprise or for separate subgroups. In the animation it is possible to test the effects of decisions related to personnel policy beforehand for the coming years.

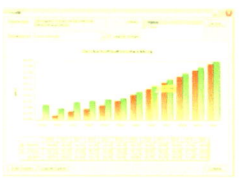

HCscore is a programm (registered trademark) of H-Faktor GmbH, Dortmund. Further information may be found at www.hcscore3.de

6.3.2 Instruments suitable for usage at the enterprise

1.	Age structure analysis (e.g. by tbs-NRW)
2.	Rough analysis checklist "Gender and age (diversity) at the enterprise"
3.	Checklist "Age Management" incl. fields of action
4.	Appreciative dialogue at the enterprise – acknowledging exchange with experience and work accomplishment discussions as the instrument for personnel management
4.a	Guidelines and qualifying workshop "Acknowledging exchange with experience"
4.b	Guidelines and qualifying workshop "Attentive work accomplishment discussion"

1. Age structure analysis

Age structure analysis is a systematic approach to the description and visual representation of current and future personnel situations which have to be attributed to the development of corporate age structure.

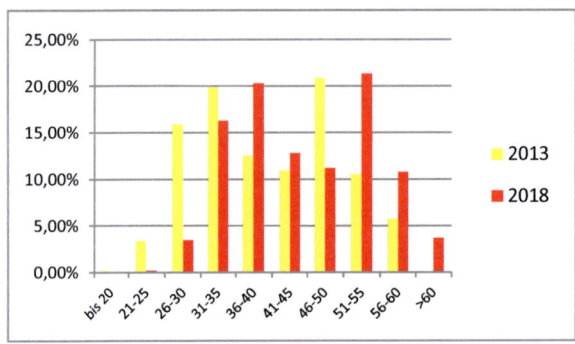

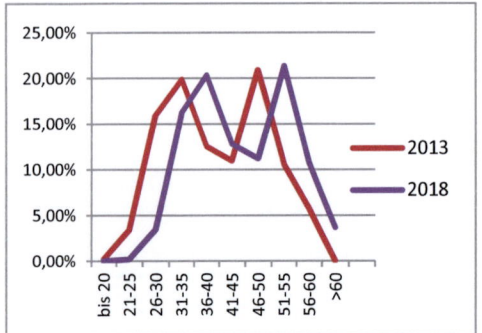

Diagram: Age structure at the enterprise in a 5-year comparison; two possible forms of representation

The quantitative representation illustrates the possible risks related to personnel policy at an early stage. The selection of possible range of tasks is provided with exemplary central questions.

- Recruiting
  Is the sufficient number of positions for trainees, apprentices etc. available?
  What new workers are planned to be employed?

Do reasonable alternatives exist for the previously usual employment of younger specialists as e.g. experienced staff or those returning to work (internally)?

- Fluctuation

  What provisions are made so that specialists with many years of professional experience were bound to the enterprise for a longer term?

- Aspects of work ability

  Is the enterprise oriented so that in the future more employees wanted or had to work until reaching the age of 65?

  Is the corporate personnel placement/personnel development strategy organized so that groups of middle-aged or elderly persons who have worked for a long time at working places with "age-critical" loads would have more performance limitations and chronic diseases?

  Do we have employees who haven't participated in further training measures for a long time and who must embrace the coming changes for the active cooperation?

- Knowledge transfer

  How is the knowledge exchange between young and older employees organized in daily routine: through tandems with younger and older employees, through supervision of young professionals by experienced employees, through stronger consideration of groups with mixed age at corporate workshops, working groups, project teams, committees?

- …

These various instruments are available for direct use, as download or for a user fee or for the purchase in the internet.

One of the instruments which were developed with public funding[14] should be briefly presented further.

[14] The development of version 3.0 was funded by the EU Social Fund and the Ministry of Labour, Integration and Social Affairs NRW (MAIS) within the framework of the project "Information and

DemografieKompass

➔ http://www.demobib.de/bib/index,id,1689.html

"With the help of the DemografieKompass of TBS [Technology Consulting Center of German Trade Unions in NRW] you can evaluate in several minutes the age structure and the qualifications of the employees at the enterprise or you can start a detailed age structure analysis. A curve illustrates the age structure at the enterprise. With a further mouse click you can start the forecast function.

In the graphic evaluation you may observe the real time during which changes occur which are related to the ageing of personnel. You can show and hide further information related to the groups of employees in the graphic evaluation. It is up to you to decide how far you look into the future. The DemografieKompass makes it possible for you to create forecasts of the corporate age structure in yearly stages. You can use the DemografieKompass with basic functions online in the browser. In addition thereto the freeware for Windows offers comprehensive possibilities to import data from Excel and other programs and to create a detailed forecast concerning the corporate age structure.

Check with the help of the DemografieKompass

- how the share of older employees will change over the next few years,
- when and how many employees will retire,
- how strong the fluctuation influences the personnel
- how the tomorrow's age structure will look like if you hire new employees
- adapt the graphic representation of results according to your desires
- use the static key figures from the table with results".

---

service network Demographic Change". The TBS NRW has conceptually managed and co-financed the development. The version 2.0 of the **DemografieKompass was** funded by the EU Social Fund and the Ministry of Labour, Health and Social Affairs NRW (MAGS) within the framework of the project "demoBiB" of the TBS NRW.

The DemografieKompass can be used online; the software can also be downloaded and installed for the use at the enterprise. This is a tool for entrepreneurs, heads of human resources, works councils and staff councils as well as interested employees. The use is free of charge. Consultants and initiatives can use the DemografieKompass taking into account the Terms of use for TBS software.

2. Quick check related to the ageing- and gender-sensitive evaluation of personnel policy[15]

Many enterprises realize more and more the specific effects of the demographic development at their enterprise/their plant/their organization. The quick check makes it possible to perform the first evaluation of the initial situation related to personnel policy taking into account age, gender, qualification and health.

Please answer the following questions related to the central fields of action of the management concerning the organization of the demographic change at the enterprise.

In the fields where your answer is "not applicable" there is probably the need for action. In order to determine what you can do specifically further examination of related topics is required, for example through in-depth analysis, the development of the active accomplishment strategy or similar.

---

[15] The basis of this checklist is the "Quick check of the demographic change at the enterprise" which was developed in the Project "DemoKomp" (Demography Competence), which was funded by the initiative New Quality of Work (INQA). For background and for the online self-test see http://www.inqa-demographic-check.de/selbsttest.php

1) Personnel recruiting and development	Rather applicable	Rather not applicable
We know the **structural data** of employees at our enterprise according to age, gender and qualification.		
We take into account the **age and gender composition** by our decisions concerning the personnel policy.		
We consider the specific **strong points** of women and older employees in our employment and personnel development policy.		
We attempt (using corresponding incentives) to bind **specialists and management** to our enterprise.		
We consider the change of physical, spiritual and social competences of employees who grow older and have a concept for ageing-appropriate activities/**professional careers.**		
We have no problem to attract **young professionals** to get education as well as experienced specialists to our enterprise.		
We have a good image in the region in our branch and we are regarded as an **attractive employer.**		
2) Work organization and work design		
We offer **professional perspective** at our enterprise to employees of all age groups.		

We employ our employees according to their **capabilities** and their **health**.		
The **activities** and the work processes are organized so that they could be executed also by older employees until their retirement.		
We prompt our employees to help us organize their **workplace** and **work processes**, e.g. through promotion of improvement suggestions.		
We attempt to organize the work places of our employees flexibly (part-time, working time accounts etc.) and take into account various life situations (parental leaves/nursing care etc.).		

3) Qualification and development of competences		
We know the **strong and the weak points** of our employees and we try to keep them up to date with their knowledge through corresponding qualification.		
We offer to all the employees regardless of their age to **enhance** their **competences** e.g. through workshops, manufacturer trainings or in-company trainings.		
We take care that **further training measures** were in line with various learning needs and capabilities of the employees.		
We ensure that in case of changes of activities and before the dismissal of employees the **competences**		

were retained for the enterprise.		
4) Management and corporate culture		
We promote the **work climate** which is oriented at the **appreciation** of different groups of employees (older and younger, women and men, foreigners, skilled, semi-skilled, specialists, management staff…).		
At our enterprise all the employees are **treated fairly** by the superiors.		
We sensitize our superiors regularly for the specific concerns of the older employees.		
Our superiors promote the **dialogue between older and younger employees,** e.g. through the creation of teams with mixed age.		
5) Health and labour protection		
At our enterprise frequent health problems or accident hotspots do not occur.		
At our enterprise we have an ageing- and gender-sensible evaluation of risks.		
We regularly check physical, psychic, mental and social requirements (loads), individual and organizational resources and the possibilities for accomplishment (stresses) of work.		

We offer to our employees support for the preservation and promotion of their health and well-being (measures of health promotion).		
We have a functioning health management.		
The rehabilitation after the illness is regulated and employees with limited capacities if possible receive the adapted range of activities/working requirements.		

3. Checklist "Aging management"

The checklist on aging management puts forward questions to the company, which can be answered by the management or together with the employees:

- Is the question important for us?
- Do we have a solution?
- For which goal do we want to implement which measures?
- …

Some possible goal statements can be formulated as examples, they should be formulated specifically for the company.

(1)   What should managers know about "aging management"?

1. Age structure of enterprises - today and tomorrow
2. Concept of workability
3. Workability and economy
4. Aging and productivity
5. Aging and Health
6. Aging and development of mental abilities
7. Aging and performance
8. Aging and learning
9. Aging and autonomy of performance
10. Age Management Tools
11. Prevention of age discrimination

(2)   Keywords and key questions for aging management

Awareness

➢ Our executives are aware of the challenges of demographic change for the labor market due to the aging of the workforce and the need for younger workers.
- What is our age profile today, and in 5 and 10 years from now?
- What is the optimal age structure for us?
- Do we need older, experienced workers?
- Are there problems due to early retirement?
- How do we attract younger workers?
- How do the generations work together?
- …

Settings / attitude

➢ Our executives have a positive attitude towards older people and their operational capability and value their knowledge and competencies.
- What are our attitudes towards older people?
- Are there differences in the attitudes between managers, employees, professional groups or departments?
- Do we know cases of age discrimination?
- What can we do to change attitudes?
- Does our awareness grow with the help of older people?

Responsibilities of managers / management

➢ The managers feel personally committed to the employment and promotion of work ability of people of all ages.
- What does the diversity of the workforce mean for older workers?
- How seriously do we take will individual differences into account?
- How can the work assignments be organized for the different generations?
- Do we have a life-cycle model in management?
- Do we mobilize all of us individual strengths?
- What are the different solutions and adjustments needed by each age group?

Active Aging Strategy

➢ In our organization the issues of lifelong learning, cooperation of all generations, equal opportunities for professional development and employment of older workers have seen significant improvement. For these purposes we have a systematic staff development strategy.
- Do we have a systematic staff development with the corresponding models?
- Do we have an active strategy?
- How do we perform evaluation?
- How is lifelong learning supported?
- How is cooperation of generations supported?
- …

Workability, motivation and interest to work

➢ Workability (health, motivation and expertise) of our older employees is so high that they are willing and able to work longer that/until retirement or the age of retirement.
- What skills does our company need?
- How is the workability of our older employees?
- How can we promote workability at work?
- How can we motivate experienced employees to stay longer?
- What effect does the aging of our own executives have on their attitudes towards older employees?
- Do we offer part-time opportunities for older employees?
- …

Competences

➢ Our executives have agreed that active promotion of workability of all employees is a key task. The expertise of the staff, including the implicit knowledge and the transfer of knowledge, needs to be preserved.
- What knowledge do our older employees have/need?
- What is the value of experience and implicit knowledge?
- IS there any willingness for lifelong learning?
- Do we support our staff in learning?

- Do we overly encumber older workers with new tasks?
- Do we have concrete plans to pass on the knowledge and experience?
- Do we appreciate talented staff?
- Do we value the human capital in our company?
- …

Work organization and working environment

➢ Work organization, work requirements, working hours and working environment to fit the needs of the employees of all ages.
- Do we know how to adapt work processes to the aging process?
- Do older employees have a say in their work?
- How should the workload change with aging?
- How can we adapt the work to aging?
- Are the work changes acceptable for all?
- Is the work organized in such way that all work groups can be productive?
- Do we know that managers are responsible for overload or absenteeism?
- …

A good life

➢ We treat all employees, particularly older employees, with respect and appreciation. The retirement shall be dignified.
- Do we respect older employees?
- How can we improve the quality of life of older employees?
- How can we support the retirement?
- How do we ensure dignified life after leaving work?
- Do we have contact with our former employees?
- Do we offer support to former employees?
- …

4. Appreciative Dialogues in the company - appreciative experience exchange and Mindful Workability conversations as an instrument of human resource management

The central tool of personnel management is communication. Discussions are constantly held with staff/employees. However, impromptu conversations or meetings do not ensure systematic learning and development at work.

For a humane quality of work, that is enjoyable, healthy and productive - and manageable all through the retirement age, alignment of HR policies in aspects of health, well-being and workability is needed. Workplace health promotion can only be successfully achieved if managers are able to make decisions for both health-friendly conditions and themselves contribute to ensuring well-being. This necessarily includes the perception of the expertise of employees regarding their work in the form of participatory development processes.

The necessary instruments and interview techniques can be learned; genuine, appreciative attitude, as well as the appropriate supportive behavior, is the reinforcing element of a respectful personal approach.

For the purposes of appreciative dialogues on well-being, health and workability the corresponding requirements are put forward to supervisors to hold systematic discussions with all employees.

Different discussions are offered for two different key groups at enterprises:

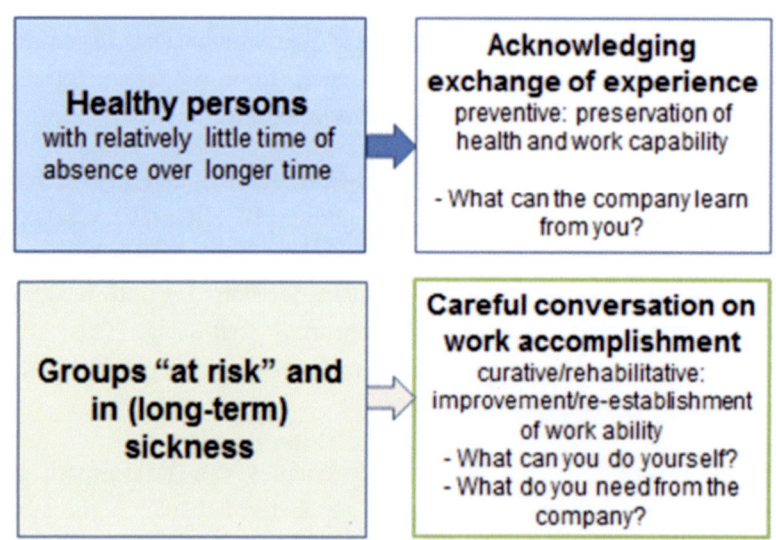

"Systematic" has two meanings in this context:

- on the one hand, the discussions follow the guideline with the most important subjects so that comparability is ensured,
- on the other, the topics of conversations in the company /by managers are evaluated in order to draw conclusions for improvements in work organization and take appropriate measures.

Both forms of conversation pursue the objectives:

- Systematic Personal Care and upkeep/increase of the value of relations in the company;
- Raising credible mutual awareness and recognition of the well-being resources in the company;
- Systematic evaluation of the evidence from these conversations for collective actions that improve the health of the company.

Appreciative dialogues are conversations in which the executives, according to the motto "He who asks is leading", encourages description and assessment of well-being resources and (potential) stress factors, including discussion of solutions or suggestions for enhancing workability. The task of the management is to activate the dialog by asking questions and also in active listening to gain more understanding of the others.

The following overview outlines the core elements of the dialogues:

	Appreciative exchange of experiences (AE)	Mindful labor-management conversation (ABW)
Promotion/ care intention	Express interest and jointly create opportunities that support conditions for high workability and to offer support for the future.	Adjust what you have to offer to ensure further workability.
Attitude and messages to employees in conversation	"To learn form you and to preserve/expand resources for the future"	"To keep you at work and to start and enact common initiatives for improvement and recovery to that end"
Dialogue tools	Six key questions to identify resources and load factors as well as possible solutions	The two key questions in four funding areas (health, skills, working conditions, working environment)
Content	• *What do you like - most - at work?* • *What bothers and burdens you - the most?* • *If you were in my position, what would be the first thing you*	*What can you do to recover/ maintain workability?* *What you need on the part of the company?* Each of the development areas:

	improve? • *What are you most proud of as a staff member of our company?* • *What, in your opinion, does the company do for the health of employees?* • *Can you perform until the statutory retirement age (for younger employees – for the next few years)? If so, how can we support that? - If not, what needs to change?*	• Health • Working conditions • Professional development and training • Working climate
Taking seriously the views and suggestions	a) Creating a memo b) Evaluation of meeting notes: list of company's Strengths/Resources and Weaknesses/Difficulties	a) Creating a needs protocol b) Review of individual realization and support options
Result and impact	a) Steering decisions for the preservation and communication of existing resources and changes in work loads b) Turning-to and recognition of employees as "company's own consultants "	a) Steering decisions for the restoration and promotion of work ability. b) Perceiving and taking into account personal needs and concerns.
Inputs	a) 30 - x minutes per person. b) Evaluation and conclusion round by executives	a) 30 - x minutes per person. b) Session "workability promoting" by executives

The stated aim is that the executives who lead those dialogues are systematically given the opportunity to conduct pleasant conversations. Thus the well-being of managers themselves can also be positively influenced.

Literature

- *Geißler, H.; Bökenheide, T; Schlünkes, H.; Geißler-Gruber, B. (2007):* Faktor Anerkennung. Betriebliche Erfahrungen mit wertschätzenden Dialogen. Frankfurt/New York.

- *Gruber, Brigitta; Frevel, Alexander (2010):* Wertschätzende Dialoge im Betrieb. Führung als Co-Produzent von Wohlbefinden, in: ergomed – Zeitschrift für arbeitsmedizinische Praxis und betriebliches Gesundheitsmanagement: 34. Jg., H. 1, S. 12-20.

4.a Guidance and Qualification Seminar "appreciative experience exchange"

The appreciative experience exchange (AE) is a 1-day (up to 1.5) training.

The target group is managers (those with personal responsibility).

Draft theme plan

	Round of introductions; orientation
	<ul><li>Brief introduction to the appreciative experience exchange (AE)</li><li>Practice of AE in pairs (approximately 2 x 45')</li></ul>
	<ul><li>Exchange of experiences on AE</li><li>Input: Health-promoting leadership (Appreciative relationships, social & organizational resources, strengths / weaknesses of the company, psychological employment contract); concept of workability</li></ul>

• Input: evaluation of AE results
• Exercise: Anonymous evaluation of the strengths and weaknesses and localization of in-house workability
• Exercise: Evaluation Workshop - Exemplary development of measures based on the strengths/weaknesses list.
• Dealing with difficult interview situations - Exercises (collegial case advice)

4.b Guidance and Qualification Seminar "Mindful Workability conversation"

The Mindful Workability conversation (AAB) is in a one-day training. A recess of about 1.5 hours is suggested in connection with the appreciative experience exchange training.

The target group is managers (those with personal responsibility) as well as members of the company social management, health and safety committees or integration management teams.

Draft theme plan

Round of introductions; orientation
• Input: Concept of workability • Self-awareness: labor-management index • Input: Health-promoting leadership (Appreciative relationships, social & organizational resources, strengths / weaknesses of the company, psychological employment contract)

- Input: Integration management, legal aspects and operational arrangements

- Exercise on communication skills with collegial case advice

- Exercise: Evaluation Workshop - Exemplary development of measures on the basis of conversations and implemented measures

7. Creative Age Management Strategies for SMEs in the Baltic Sea Region (developed within the project "Best Agers" with the assistance of the European Union and the German Federal Ministry of Transport, Building and Urban Development)

By comparing the country studies in the Baltic Sea Region we can see a clear dependence on the social and economic situation. The Nordic countries (especially Finland), the United Kingdom, and Germany are the most economically developed to overcome the challenges of demographic change. For historical reasons, there are still significant differences between the countries analysed, e.g. in the standard of living, economic strength, health care situation, infrastructure, political stability and/or working conditions.

It turns out, however, that those countries with fewer problems related to demographic change started early to develop integrated policies to address the challenges.

The analysis of the data and the summarised information in the country studies show a hologram: each element of the system reflects the qualities of the entirety. This means in simple terms:

- The countries which have a strong strategy for coping with demographic change generally show more positive values with respect to individual indicators, such as the participation rate of older people and women, higher birth rates, higher job satisfaction, higher education rates.

- On the other hand: those countries which are expected to have a bigger problem with demographic structure change have – among other factors – lower participation in education and more stressful work situations. And they usually have no clear political strategy.

The **good news** is: Demographic change can be altered in its effects and designed in its consequences.

Different Levels of Preparedness and Range of Integrated Approaches

The different strategies of the Baltic Sea Region countries range from the perception of the problem to challenge demographic change up to integrated policies.

Many of the programmes and projects are comparable, dealing with limited goals (awareness raising), limited target groups (employees 50+, apprentices), and/or narrow approaches (health promotion, or further training in specific technologies).

Most measures of companies are oriented in a somewhat reactive manner. Ageing of the workforce is very often perceived as a (enormous) challenge. The approaches are limited in their effect, as measures like decreasing work demands or enhancing individual resources (skills, individual prevention, and healthy lifestyle) do not really change the working conditions in an age-appropriate and ageing-adjusted way.

There are few but impressive examples of integrated policies and actions, which exceed the threshold level of pro-active solutions. These solutions identify ageing as an opportunity and have a broad life-course approach. Wallin and Hussi[16] indicate a large variability in age management approaches, varying from organisations without any age awareness to organisations who view ageing as a challenge or as an opportunity, to more advanced organisations that provide equal opportunities. The most developed organisations are characterized by proactive measures (Figure 1).

---

[16] Marjo Wallin / Tomi Hussi (2011): Best Practices in Age Management – Evaluation of Organisation Cases, FIOH, Helsinki

Establishing a Good Balance between Individual's and Social's Needs

From a broad perspective mainly the Nordic states pursue integrated policy approaches with the focus on improving opportunities for employees, employers and society. The life-course approach is characterised by a simultaneous consideration of both individual and social opportunities.

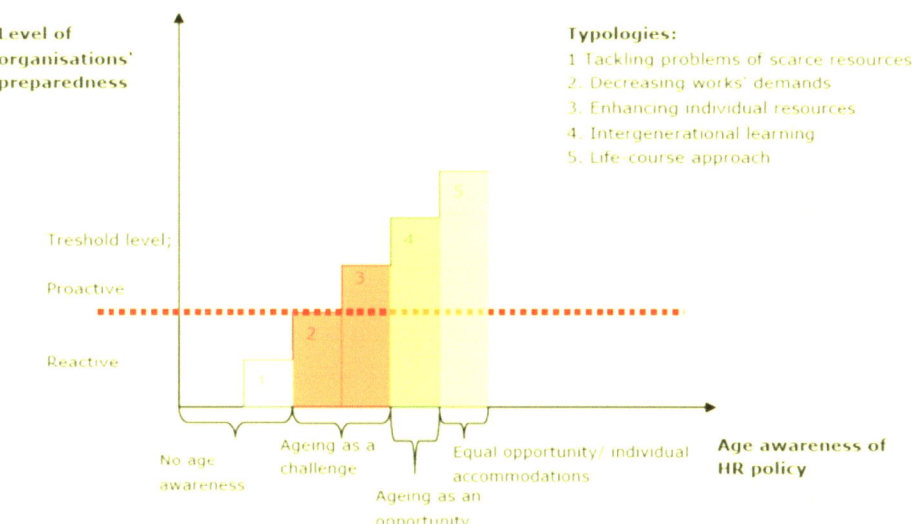

At the state level, there are coordinated policies to encourage individuals and families. Society's attitude towards the elderly and towards ageing is promoted accordingly. Particularly pronounced in these societies is the offer to remove social burdens on families. In Norway and Finland for example there is a flexible pension system which – instead of reducing pension-income in the case of early employment termination – provides bonuses for the extension of working life. This also applies to the healthcare system which is oriented towards prevention.

Research and development in these countries provides significant contributions to the active support for companies through targeted promotion programmes. The examples of different programmes built on each other in Finland show the feasibility and the necessity of longer-term development programmes which create a consistent policy. The concept of work ability, which is defined as the balance between work demands and individual resources, reaches both the corporate and the individual level. Since both the work requirements (technology, organisation, working hours, etc.) as well as the person (age, health, competence) may change over time, it is necessary to preserve the stability of work ability for the duration of the working life. This cannot be done by individuals on their own – people and businesses must work together so that the "House of Work Ability" is built on firm bedrock.

In **Finland** the age management training of managers not only increases the awareness of diversity management issues, but also supports the corporate design of the job requirements.

In **Norway**, at the Centre for Senior Policy, there are state-funded advisors to assist with the corporate implementation of the employment extension.

In **Germany** there is an upcoming number of collective agreements handling the demographic change. Best known is the agreement in the Chemical Industry which among other aspects prescribes the implementation of an age structure analysis and installs a self-financed fund for operational measures.

Approaches on Company Level

Special Focus on SME

SMEs, which account for 99,8 % of all companies in Europe, employ two-thirds of all employees. In other words, a third of all workers are employed in only 0,2 % of the enterprises. Small companies - which in Europe number at least 92 % of all SMEs – employ less than 10 employees on average.

The specific structural situation is characterised by the fact that the owner frequently works operationally him- or herself. There are no staff positions for the various tasks and small capacities for strategic projects. Although there are many companies realising product innovation there is a lack concerning process innovation. Activities in the fields of Human Resource Development, Occupational Health Management, or systematic training get less attention in terms of time, money and creativity. Indeed, many of these companies feel the growing shortage of young talents, but for individual businesses demographic change seems to be a rare event.

Consequently the described situation leads to the fact that there are very few examples of good practice projects from these types of establishments. In addition, the quality of the description is not always meaningful enough for an instructive and transferable image.

Examples of Companies' Good Practices

Companies' offers to reduce the labour requirements of older employees focus on the reduction of working time. They take changing capacities and skills of ageing individuals into consideration. They are often combined with measures to support healthiness.

Up to now there are only few companies in Europe that have implemented a clearly noticeable increase in the retirement age of their workforce. The most impressive examples are introduced shortly.

AgeMaster by Abloy Oy, Finland

Targets:	Keeping the experienced lock-making workers in the company up to their retirement age and supporting them by various health and job-related training services. Those older than 58 years joined the AgeMaster Club. AgeMasters were given additional free days aimi
Concept:	Additional free days increasing by age (from 6 days/year for 58 years old employees up to 14 d/y for 63 plus) and voluntary health promotion.
Prerequisites:	Permanent contract and annual health and fitness tests by occupational health services.
Agreements:	Max 3 free consecutive days, agreed by the supervisor.
Results:	Retirement ages increased by about 3 years.

Senior Policy in Sandnes Municipality, Norway

Targets: Comprehensive programme in 3-levels; reduced workload; extra investments for personal and workplace improvements;
Focus group: employees aged 62 – 66 years old.

Concept: Reducing working hours from 90 % (62 years old employees) to 80 % (64+) at full pay (100 % salary).

Prerequisites: Reduced workload should normally be organised as fixed weekly reductions in working hours and tasks. When enrolled in the programme, it will last until retirement and cannot be combined with early age pension (AFP). Special regulations have been created for teachers to decrease their workload, starting at age of 55 years.

Agreements: Annual reporting
Work environment survey (degree of satisfaction) every second year.

Results: Halving sick leave for employees aged 60 years +
Changed attitudes towards older workers
Retention of Competence, delayed recruitment needs, positive branding for Sandnes Municipality as employer.

The 80-90-100 programme by Vattenfall, Sweden

Targets: Longer work careers with stepwise increase retirement age up to 67 (65-67-70), decreasing work load by reducing the work time for 58+, decreasing sickness absence, transfer of tacit knowledge of experienced technical staff.

Concept: 80-90-100 = working time 80 %, salary 90 %, pension entitlement 100 %.

Prerequisites: Open for everybody – pilot 6 months – employer's decision whether back to old or wish to continue.

Results: 25 % of the workforce aged 58+ used the new schedule; it did not hinder organisational effectiveness because of better arrangements of the tasks, it increased motivation and vitality, and reduced stress. It contributed to an increase in average retirement ages to 63 (+ 3 years).Retirement ages increased by about 3 years.

Collective Agreement on Demographic Change and Intergenerational Fairness – Verkehrsbetriebe Hamburg-Holstein (Public Transport), Germany

Targets: Adaptation of work to individuals
Measures to stabilize the balance of working capacity on all levels of work ability

Concept: a) Ergonomics: design of the bus drivers workplaces after secured ergonomics findings: pause control, avoidance of night work
b) Reduction of working time by release days:
b1) individually to 55 years as needed,
b2) from 56 years old get 4 days/year, 59: 6, 62: 8, 64+: 10
c) Appreciative dialogues with each employee:
c1) appreciative exchange of experience (about 90 % of all employees; annually),
c2) attentive work ability dialogue / integration of long-term sick/disabled (10 %; if required)
d) Promoting professional and personal skills
e) Health promotion (prevention, cure, rehabilitation)
f) Preparing for post-work life.

Agreements: Evaluation with the Work Ability Index and work ability dialogues with the employees (Occupational Health Service)
Annual analysis of the age structure, assessment of workload

Results: The agreement was concluded in June 2012

Recommendations

To become effective, all policies and actions have to be oriented towards the aim to install an excellent (occupational) well-being in productive enterprises. Employees have to be supported so that they are able, willing and allowed to work until retirement age (or longer).

Integrated Policies of Actors, Clear Levels of Approaches and Responsibilities, Concerted Actions (Magic-Box)

Successful strategies for coping with demographic change should not be singular approaches. They should involve an ensemble of policies and measures of different groups of actors in different, in different fields of action, with divergent ranges of perception, and with distinct levels of approaches for problem solving.

Figure 3: Magic box for integrated policies to cope with the challenges and opportunities of the demographic change

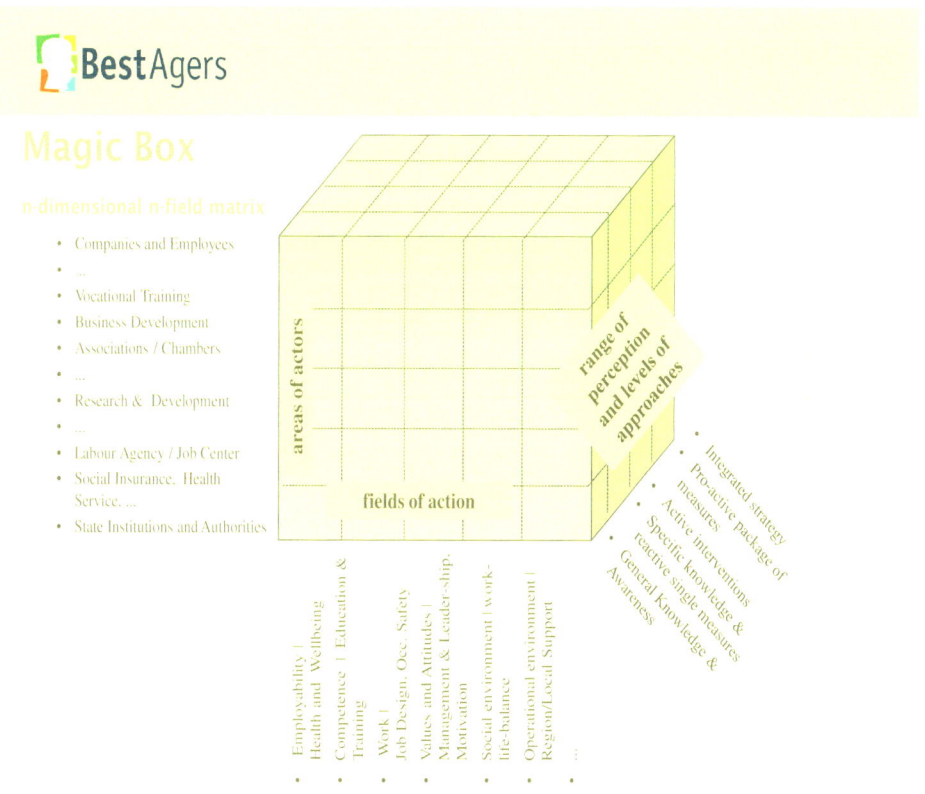

The 3-dimensional matrix of different actors, fields of action, and levels (intensities) of approaches will lead to sufficient solutions of the problems when the approaches, measures and instruments are aligned with each other.

The Magic Box may be a tool to show which actor works launches which actions (e.g. campaigns, promotion measures, active work design, increasing the ability to work) in which action field. The matrix can be used for visualisation, planning and evaluation of policies. It may be a tool to check or to verify the completeness and quality of actions as well as to identify "white spots" of actors and/or of actions, too.

Descriptions of successful approaches could be based on this structure and explain, if possible, to what extent the approaches correspond to the ideal of integrated policies. The Magic Box could also be used for programme planning at the enterprise, intermediate, regional, national or European level, if the individual categories are clearly identified and differentiated.

IMPORTANT QUESTIONS FOR AN EFFECTIVE AGE-/GENERATION-/LIFE-COURSE-MANAGEMENT

- Are the people/employees able to work until retirement age (or longer)? ✤ Health, competence, working conditions ...

→ **How can we support them?**

- Are the people/employees **willing** to work until retirement age? ✤ Values, attitudes, motivation, financial situation ...

→ **How can we win them to participate?**

- Are the people/employees **allowed** to work well, happy and healthy for a long time?
- ✤ Operational environment, society/policy

→ **How can we create an enabling environment?**

STRENGTHEN INDIVIDUAL'S AND COMPANY'S SELF-OBSERVATION AND SELF-MANAGEMENT

Asking the people:
- What can you do by yourself?
- What do you need from the company
  to support your work ability?

Asking the company:
- What can you do by yourself?
- What do you need from third parties
  to support work ability in the business?
- ➔ Changing the organisational structure, shapening age-adjusted working conditions

AGE MANAGEMENT STRATEGY – SUITABLE TO SMES
Work demand should be adjusted to employee's resources

Empowering persons and optimising the processes to support well-being = productivity at work needs

- Transition from a „Culture of early retirement" towards a → „Culture of prolonging well-being in working life"
- Knowledge about ageing and health
- Attitudes towards diversity including older workers
- Managing operational work ability: prevention, behavioural and environmental change, age-appropriate work design
- Appreciative Dialogues and participation in change processes

SUPPORTING AGE MANAGEMENT
- Operational Level
What managers need to know about age and aging

- Aging and productivity
- Aging and health
- Aging and performance
- Aging and attitudes (participation)
- Aging and learning
- Aging and age-appropriate work design (→ Measures & Interventions)
- Prevention of age discrimination (→ Diversity Management)

- Age structures and forecast the future development
- Qualification demands (in respect to technological and market development)
- Dimensions of aging
- Concept of life-course
- Concept of work ability
- Aging and work design
- Age Management Tools (e.g. Appreciative Exchange of Experience, attentive work ability dialogue)

SUPPORTING AGE MANAGEMENT
- Intermediaries Level

BDO, Chambers; Social Insurance; Labour Office; Local Authorities
make resources of well-trained consultants available

- Process monitoring with expert advice
- Training/Coaching individuals and companies
- Facilitation of action planning to agreements by consensus of the corporate players → development programmes
- Providing specialized advice for job design, health-promoting leadership, working hours (e.g. shift patterns), relief programs for the older workers, etc.

- Policy & State Institutions
- Financing of training programmes for consultants and trainers
- Establishment of departments/institutes of generation related work including internship in SMEs
- R & D programmes for SMEs to transfer/adapt/applicate existing knowledge

Working until 65+?

Positive Reforms first – negative later!
- **First,** improve the working lives so that people are able, willing and allowed to work longer
- Promoting work ability and work well-being by evidence-based concepts - integrated activities on all floors of work ability house
- **Later,** reducing early retirement and raising the retirement age
- Working longer / up to 65+ / is implemented in workplaces, not in the political arena
- Work demand should be adjusted to employee resources to help to ensure better functional ability for people also years after their retirement

For further information, see: Arbeit und Zukunft e. V.

8. Contact details of advisory offices and supporting institutions

8.1 SME Support Network Hanseatic Parliament

Secretariat

Hanseatic Parliament, Blankeneser Landstraße 7, D-22587 Hamburg, Germany, Phone +49 (0) 40 82 24 47 0, Fax +49 (0) 40 82 24 47 22, email: info@hanse-parlament.eu, Internet: www.hanse-parlament.eu

Members

The Chamber of Craftmanship and Enterprise in Białystok, ul. Warszawska 6, PL-15-950 Białystok, Poland, Phone +48 85/743 54 03, Fax +48 85/743 61 41, email: izba@rzemioslo.bialystok.pl, Internet: www.rzemioslo.bialystok.pl

Braunschweig-Lüneburg-Stade Chamber of Skilled Crafts and Small Businesses, Friedenstr. 6, D-21335 Lüneburg, Germany, Phone +49/4131/712 - 0, Fax +49/4131/447 24, email: info@hwk-bls.de, Internet: www.hwk-bls.de

Brest Branch of the Belarusian Chamber of Commerce and Industry, Gogol str. 13, BY-224030 Brest, Belarus, Phone +375/162 21 90 70, Fax +375/162 21 78 85, email: tpp@brest.by, Internet: www.cci.by

Hungarian Association of Craftsmen Corporations, Kàlmán Imre u. 20, H-1054 Budapest, Hungary, Phone +36/1/269 29 50, Fax +36/1/269 29 57, email: rettich@iposz.hu, Internet: www.iposz.hu

Kujawsko-Pomorska Chamber of Craft and SME's, ul. Piotrowskiego 11, PL-85 098 Bydgoszcz, Poland, Phone +48 52/322 12 76, Fax +48 52/322 14 23, email: sekretariat@izbarzem.pl, Internet: www.izbarzem.pl

Cottbus Chamber of Skilled Crafts and SME's, Altmarkt 17, D-03046 Cottbus, Germany, Phone +49 (0) 3 55/78 35 - 0, Fax +49 (0) 3 55/78 35 – 281, email: hwk@hwk-cottbus.de, Internet: www.hwk-cottbus.de

Dresden Chamber of Skilled Crafts and Small Businesses, Am Lagerplatz 8, D-01099 Dresden, Germany, Phone +49 (0) 3 51/46 40 30, Fax +49 (0) 3 51/471 91 88, email: jana.westphaelinger@hwk-dresden.de, Internet: www.hwk-dresden.de

Pomeranian Chamber of Handicrafts for SME's, ul. Piwna 1/2, PL-80-831 Gdańsk, Poland, Phone +48 58/301 84 41, Fax +48 58/301 79 31, email: biuro@pomorskaizba.com.pl, Internet: www.pomorskaizba.com.pl

Gomel Department of the Belarusian Chamber of Commerce and Industry, 21 Irininskaya Str, BY-246017 Gomel, Belarus, Phone + 375 232 70 18 61, Fax + 375 232 71 32 35, email: vyd@ccigomel.by

Hamburg Chamber of Skilled Crafts and Small Businesses, Holstenwall 12, D-20355 Hamburg, Germany, Phone +49/40/359 05 - 236, Fax +49/40/359 05 307, email: halbers@hwk-hamburg.de, Internet: www.hwk-hamburg.de

Ost- und Mitteleuropa Verein e.V., Dr. Hanno Stöcker, Ferdinandstr. 36, D-20095 Hamburg, Germany, Phone +49 40 33 89 45, Fax +49 40 32 35 78, email: stocker@o-m-v.org, Internet: www.o-m-v.com

Företagarna Kalmar län Service AB, Björn Langberg, Drottning Margaretas väg 32, SE-39246 Kalmar, Phone +46 702200716, email: bjorn.langberg@trebema.se, Internet: www.foretagarna.se

Kaliningrad region Handicraft Chamber, ul. Gorkogo 69, RU-236029 Kaliningrad, Russia, Phone +7 4012/96 54 31, Fax +7 4012/96 54 31, email: popov@business-zel.ru

Kaliningrad Regional Economic Development Agency, 1, Geologicheskaya str., RU-236000 Kaliningrad, Russia, Phone +7 4012 53086364, Fax +7 4012 53 08 51, email: aignatyev@list.ru, Internet: www.kaliningrad-rda.org

Kaliningrad Chamber of Commerce and Industry, 20 Vatutina Str., RU-236010 Kaliningrad, Russia, Phone +7 (4012) 590 650, +7 911 4693529, email: maximova@kaliningrad-cci.ru, Internet: www.kaliningrad-cci.ru

Chamber of Crafts and SME in Katowice, Plac Wolności 12, PL-40-078 Katowice, Poland, Phone +48 (32) 259 62 61, Fax +48 (32) 258 87 38,
email: izba@ir.katowice.pl, Internet: www.ir.katowice.pl

Chamber of Crafts and SME in Kielce, ul. Warszawska 34, PL-25-312 Kielce, Poland, Phone +48 41 344 76 53, Fax +48 41 344 9379,
email: prezes@izbarzemieslnicza.pl, Internet: www.izbarzemieslnicza.pl

IBC Innovationsfabrikken (Innovation Factory), Birkemosevej 1, DK-6000 Kolding, Denmark, Phone +45 51 95 25 87,
email: pscz@ibc.dk, Internet: www.ibc.dk

Handicraft Chamber of Ukraine, Shovkovuchna str., 32/34 office 48, UA-01024 Kyiv, Ukraine, Phone +380444657080, Mob +380985624444,
email: m.popovich@ukrrp.org, Internet: www.ukrrp.org

Kyiv Chamber of Commerce and Industry, 55 B.Khmelnytskyi Str., UA-01601 Kyiv, Ukraine, Phone +38 044 482 04 34, Fax +38 044 482 04 35,
email: info@kiev-chamber.org.ua, Internet: www.kiev-chamber.org.ua

Handicraft Chamber Leningrad Region, ul. Bolshaja Monetnaja 16, Office centre No. 1, 5. floor, Office 3, RU-197101 St. Petersburg, Russia, Phone +7/812/3365017,
email: parus-l@rambler.ru

The Craft Chamber of Lodz, ul. Moniuszki 8, PL-90-111 Łódź, Poland, Phone +48 42/632 55 81 Fax +48 42/632 37 76,
email: irlodz@home.pl, Internet: www.irlodz.home.pl

Handicraft and Small Business Chamber Lublin, ul. Rynek 2, PL-20-111 Lublin, Poland, Phone +48 81/532 80 - 11, Fax +48 81/532 29 - 25,
email: izba@izba.lublin.pl, Internet: www.izba.lublin.pl

Belarusian Chamber of Commerce and Industry, ul. Kommunisticheskaja 11, BY-220029 Minsk, Belarus, Phone +375 / 172 907 258, Fax +375 / 172 907 248,
email: dubova@cci.by, Internet: www.cci.by

Minsk Department of the Belarussian Chamber of Commerce and Industry, Y. Kolasa Str. 65, BY-220213 Minsk, Berlarus, Phone/Fax +375 172 895 681, email: tppm@tppm.by, Internet: www.cci.by

Mogilev Branch of Belarusian Chamber of Commerce and Industry, Vul. Pershamayskaya 71, Dom Savetau, of.802, BY-212030 Mahileu, Belarus, Phone +375 222 326850 and 222 273592, Fax +375 222 327398, email: tppm@tut.by, Internet: www.cci.mogilev.by

Russian Chamber of Crafts, Skotoprogonnaja Str. 29/1, RU-109029 Moskau, Russia, Phone +7 495 678 01 02, Fax +7 495 671 47 20, email: parus7777@mtu-net.ru

Warmia and Mazury Chamber of Crafts and Small Business in Olsztyn, ul. Prosta 38, PL-10-029 Olsztyn, Poland, Phone +48/89/527 61 88, Fax +48/89/527 50 45, email: biuro@izbarzem.olsztyn.pl, Internet: www.izbarzem.olsztyn.pl

Chamber of Crafts in Opole, ul. Katowicka 55, PL-45-061 Opole, Poland, Phone +48/77/4543173, Phone/Fax +48/77/4543173, email: info@izbarzem.opole.pl, Internet: www.izbarzem.opole.pl

Master of Crafts Norway, Postboks 5145, Majorstuen, N-0302 Oslo, Norway, Phone + 47 23 08 83 62 or +47 930 23 230, Fax +47 23 08 80 20, email: post@mesterbrev.no, Internet: www.mesterbrev.no

The Nordic Forum of Crafts, Harry Bjerkeng, Lilleakerv. 7, N-0283 Oslo, Norway, Phone +47 9093 5695, email: harry.bjerkeng@gmail.com, Internet: www.nhforum.org

Eastern Mecklenburg-Western Pomerania Chamber of Handicraft, Schwaaner Landstr. 8, D-18055 Rostock, Germany, Phone 03 81/45 49 - 0, Fax 03 81/45 49 - 139, email: info@hwk-omv.de, Internet: www.hwk-omv.de

Panevėžys Chamber of Commerce, Industry and Crafts, Respublikos g. 34, LT-35173 Panevėžys, Lithuania, Phone +370 45 46 36 87, Fax +370 45 46 22 27, email: Visvaldas.Matkevicius@chambers.lt or angelija.zokaitienė@chambers.lt, Internet: www.ccic.lt

Wielkopolska Craft Chamber in Poznan, Al. Niepodległości 2, PL-67-874 Poznań, Poland, Phone +48 61 853 78 05, Fax +48 61 852 13 16, email: sekretariat@irpoznan.com.pl, Internet: www.irpoznan.com.pl

Latvian Chamber of Crafts, Amatu iela 5, LV-1050 Riga, Latvia, Phone +371 672 130 07, Fax +371 673 585 70, email: vilnis@lak.lv

Donskaya Craft Chamber in Rostov/Don, 46/176 Voroshilovskiy prospekt, RU-344010 Rostov-on-Don, Russia, Phone/Fax +7 863 240 40 50, email: drp@aaanet.ru

Craft Chamber in Rzeszow, ul. Grunwaldzka 19, PL-35-959 Rzeszow, Poland, Phone +48 17 853 62 88, Fax +48 17 853 62 88, email: izba.rze@interia.pl, Internet: www.izba.rze.biponline.pl

Schwerin Chamber of Skilled Crafts, Friedenstr. 4 A, D-19053 Schwerin, Germany, Phone +49/385/74 17-0, Fax +49/385/71 60 51, email: e.hummelsheim@hwk-schwerin.de, Internet: www.hwk-schwerin.de

The Chamber of Handicraft Middle Pomerania in Słupsk, ul. Kowalska 1, PL-76-200 Słupsk, Poland, Phone +4859/842 60 05, Fax +4859/842 64 09, email: izba@rzemioslo.slupsk.pl, Internet: www.rzemioslo.slupsk.pl

The St. Petersburg Crafts Chamber, Mojkai 74 A, RU-190000 St. Petersburg, Russia, Phone +7812/319 93 26, Fax +7812/2728232, email: rem.palata@gmail.com, Internet: www.rpspb.ru

The Chamber of Crafts and SME in Szczecin, Al. Wojska Polskiego 78, PL-70-842 Szczecin, Poland, Phone +48 91/422 22 78, Fax +48 91/422 22 38, email: prezes@irszczecin.pl, Internet: www.irszczecin.pl

Estonian Association of Small and Medium Enterprises, Liivalaia 9, EE-10118 Tallinn, Estonia, Phone +372/641 09 20, Fax +372/641 09 16, email: evea@evea.ee, Internet: www.evea.ee

The Baltic Institute of Finland, P.O. Box 487, FI-33101 Tampere, Finland, Phone +358 3 5656 6945, Fax +358 3 5656 6252, email: esa.kokkonen@tampere.fi, Internet: www.baltic.org

The Organisation of Handicraft Businesses in Trondheim, Nardoveien 4, N-7032 Trondheim, Norway, Phone +47 92 06 04 80, email: arve.haugan@olk.no or evahaugan@yahoo.com or handverk@handverk.no, Internet: www.handverk.net

Vilnius Chamber of Commerce, Industry and Crafts, Algirdo 31, LT-03219 Vilnius, Lithuania, Phone +370/5/213 55 50, Fax +370/5/213 55 42, email: vilnius@cci.lt, Internet: www.cci.lt

The Chamber of Crafts of Mazovia, Kurpie and Podlasie Regions in Warsaw, ul. Chmielna 98, PL-00-801 Warszawa, Poland, Phone +48 22/620 50 11, Fax +48 22/620 69 64, email: izba@izbarzem-mkp.com.pl, Internet: www.izbarzem-mkp.com.pl

Small Business Chamber Warsaw, ul. Smocza 27, PL-01-048 Warszawa, Poland, Phone +48 22/838 16 10, Fax +48 22/838 35 53, email: promocja@mirip.org.pl, Internet: www.fund.org.pl

The Lower Silesian Chamber of Craft and Small and Medium-sized Businesses, Plac Solny 13, PL-50-061 Wrocław, Poland, Phone +48 71 344 87 86, Fax +48 71 343 38 32, email: sekretariat@izba.wroc.pl, Internet: www.izba.wroc.pl

8.2   SME Innovation Support Network Baltic Sea Academy

Secretariat

Baltic Sea Academy, Blankeneser Landstraße 7, D-22587 Hamburg, Germany, Phone + 49 (0) 40 82 24 47 0, Fax + 40 40 82 24 47 22, email: info@hanseparlament.eu, Internet: www.baltic-sea-academy.eu

Members

University in Bialystok, Renata Przygodzka, email: rprzygodzka@wp.pl

Brest State Technical University, ul. Moskovskaja 267, BY-224017 Brest, Belarus, Phone +375 29 6271168 or Phone/Fax +375162408374, email: liholodar@bstu.by or prorovag@mail.ru or ttc@bstu.by

University 21 non-profit limited Liability Company, Harburger Straße 4, D-21614 Buxtehude, Germany, Phone +49 4161 648 148, Fax +49 4161 648 123, email: Betzler@hs21.de, Internet: www.hs21.de

Gdansk University of Technology, ul. Narutowicza 11/12, 80-233 Gdańsk, Poland, Phone + 48 58 348 62 90, Fax + 48 58 347 18 61, email: marzena.starnawska@zie.pg.gda.pl, Internet: www.pg.gda.pl

Hanse-Parlament e.V., Blankeneser Landstr. 7, D-22587 Hamburg, Germany, Phone +49 40 822 447 0, Fax +49 40 822 447 22, email: mhogeforster@hanse-parlament.eu, Internet: www.hanse-parlament.eu

Hamburg University of Corporate Education, Zum Handwerkszentrum 1, D-21079 Hamburg, Germany, Phone +49 40 35905 566, Fax +49 40 35905 44566, email: kiedrowski@ba-hamburg.de, Internet: www.ba-hamburg.de

Hamburg Institute of International Economics, Heimhuder Straße 71, D-20148 Hamburg, Germany, Phone +49 (0)40 34 05 76 - 660, Fax +49 (0)40 34 05 76 - 776, email: stiller@hwwi.org, Internet: www.hwwi.org

Lund University, P.O. Box 117, SE–22100 Lund, Sweden, Phone +46 46 220 892, Fax +46 46 223 845, email: Per.Odenrick@design.lth.se, Internet: www.ll.lu.se

Panevezys College, Laisvės a. 23, LT-35200 Panevėžys, Lithuania, Phone +370 45 460116, email: direktorius@panko.lt or deimante.konciuviene@panko.lt, Internet: http://panko.lt/english/

Satakunta University of Applied Sciences, Tiedepuisto 3B, P.O. Box 520, FI-28601 Pori, Finland, Phone +358 2 620 32 10, Fax +358 2 620 33 00, email: matti.lahdeniemi@samk.fi or Sirpa.sandelin@samk.fi, Internet: www.samk.fi

University of Latvia, Raina Bulv. 19, LV-1586 Riga, Latvia, Phone/Fax: +371 67223984 or Mobile +371 29 136 867,
email: zzeibote@gmail.com or matiss.neimanis@lu.lv, Internet: www.lu.lv/eng

Saint-Petersburg State University of Service and Economics, Kavalergardskaya str. 7, RU-191015, Saint-Petersburg, Russia, Phone +7 (812) 577-32-19, Fax +7 (812) 610-57-38, email: ir_spbsuse@mail.ru, Internet: www.service.in.spb.ru

Hanseatic Academy of Management, ul. Kozietulskiego 6-7, PL-76-200 Słupsk, Poland, Phone +48 59 848 28 63 or 67, Fax +48 59 848 28 68,
email: kanclerz@whsz.slupsk.pl, Internet: www.whsz.slupsk.pl

Tampere University of Technology (TUT), Korkeakoulunkatu 10, FI-33720 Tampere, Finland, Phone +358 40 849 0821,
email: eu@tut.fi, Internet: www.tut.fi/en

Lithuanian University of Educational Sciences, Studentų g. 39, LT-08106 Vilnius, Lithuania, Phone +370 2790281, Fax +370 85 2790548,
email: vytas.navickas@leu.lt, Internet: www.vpu.lt

Vilnius Gediminas Technical University, Sauletekio av. 11, LT-10223 Vilnius, Lithuania, Phone +370 5 274 5018, Fax +370 5 274 5018,
email: romualdas.ginevicius@adm.vgtu.lt, Internet: www.vgtu.lt

Võru County Vacational Training Centre, Väimela, Võru vald, Võru Maakond 65566, Estonia, Phone +372 78 50 800, Fax +372 78 50 801,
email: kruusalu@vkhk.ee, Internet: www.vkhk.ee

8.3   Other supporting institutions

Arbeit und Zukunft e. V. (Work and Future), Alexander Frevel, Behringstraße 28a - Haus 1, D-22765 Hamburg. Phone +49 -40 209 139 17,
email: sekretariat@arbeitundzukunft.de, Internet: www.arbeitundzukunft.de

State Education Centre (VISC), Inta Baranovska, Vaļņu iela 2, LV-1050 Riga, Lativa, Phone +371 67350961, Fax +371 67226535,
email: inta.baranovska@visc.gov.lv, Internet: www.visc.gov.lv

Norden Association, Anders Bergström, Hantverkargatan 29, SE-104 22 Stockholm, Sweden, Phone +46 8 506 113 00, Fax +46 8 506 113 20, email: anders.bergstrom@norden.se, Internet: www.norden.se

9. Literature review

Adecco Group (2011): It's Time to Manage Age report. Adecco Group White Paper, http://www.adecco.pl/SiteCollectionDocuments/Adecco_WP_Manage_Age_2011.pdf, referred 29/11/2013.

Ageing and Mass Media: Age into focus-report, http://www.age-platform.eu/images/stories/EN/AgeIntoFocus.pdf, referred 29.11.2013.

Arbeit und Zukunft e.V. (Hrsg.)(2006): Dialoge verändern. Partizipative Arbeitsgestaltung – Voraussetzungen, Methoden und Erfahrungen für eine zukunftsfähige Arbeitsforschung. Köln

Biermann, U.; Boll, C., Reich, N.; Neubach, Stiller, S. (2013): Economic Perspectives, Qualifications and Labour Market Integration of Women in the Baltic Sea Region, M. Hogeforster (ed.): Baltic Sea Academy 9. Norderstedt, Germany.

Bogan, C.E.; English, M.J. (1994): Benchmarking for Best Practices: Winning Through Innovative Adaptation. New York: McGraw-Hill.

Brücker, Herbert; Damelang, Andreas; Wolf, Katja (2009): Labour Mobility within the EU in the Context of Enlargement and the Functioning of the Transitional Arrangements. Forecasting Potential Migration from the New Member States into the EU-15: Review of Literature, Evaluation of Forecasting Methods and Forecast Results VC/2007/0293, European Integration Consortium. Brüssel.

Bundesanstalt für Arbeitsschutz- und Arbeitsmedizin / Initiative Neue Qualität der Arbeit (Hrsg.) / Wissenschaftliche Ausarbeitung: Brigitta Gruber und Alexander Frevel (2013): Das Individuum stärken, die betriebliche Zukunft sichern. Arbeitsbewältigungs-Coaching® als Antwort auf neue Herausforderungen. 2. aktualisierte Auflage, Dortmund/Berlin.

Bundesministerium für Bildung und Forschung (2007): Bericht zur technologischen Leistungsfähigkeit Deutschlands 2007. Berlin.

Business Training Works (2013): Free Icebreakers, http://www.businesstrainingworks.com/training-resources/free-icebreakers, referred 29/11/2013.

Business Training Works (2013): Articles and Free Stuff for Training, http://www.businesstrainingworks.com/training-resources/free-articles-and-handouts, referred 29/11/2013.

Business Training Works (2013): Presentation Skills Training Resources and Articles, http://www.businesstrainingworks.com/training-resources/presentation-skills-articles, referred 29/11/2013.

Business Training Works (2002): Creative Icebreakers, Introductions, and Hellos for Teachers, Trainers, and Facilitators, Maryland: Business Training Works, http://www.businesstrainingworks.com/workshop_downloads_PDF/Icebreakers.PDF, referred 29/11/2013.

Business Training Works (2004): The Trainer's Survival Guide. Maryland: Business Training Works, http://www.leotrainer.com/tactiveteach.pdf, referred 29/11/2013

European Commission (2013): Equality pays off, http://ec.europa.eu/justice/gender-equality/equality-pays-off/index_en.htm, referred 29/11/2013.

European Commission (2013): Europa press release Equal Pay Day: Women in Europe work 59 days 'for free'. Brussels: European Commission, http://europa.eu/rapid/press-release_IP-13-165_en.htm?locale=en, referred 29/11/2013.

European Commission (2012): European Employment Observatory Review Employment Policies to Promote Active Ageing 2012, Luxembourg: Publications Office of the European Union, http://ec.europa.eu/social/main.jsp?catId=738&langId=en&pubId=6783&type=2&furtherPubs=yes, referred 29/11/2013.

European Commission (2012): Women in economic decision-making in the EU, Progress report. Luxembourg: Publications Office of the European Union, http://ec.europa.eu/justice/gender-equality/files/women-on-boards_en.pdf, referred 29/11/2013.

European Commission (2012): Demography, active ageing and pensions report. Luxembourg: Publications Office of the European Union, http://ec.europa.eu/social/main.jsp?catId=738&langId=en&pubId=6805&type=2& furtherPubs=no, referred 29/11/2013.

European Commission (2011): Europe can do better report. Warsaw, European Commission, http://ec.europa.eu/dgs/secretariat_general/admin_burden/best_practice_report/d ocs/bp_report_signature_en.pdf, referred 29/11/2013.

European Commission (2011): WES - the European network to promote women's entrepreneurship, http://ec.europa.eu/enterprise/policies/sme/promoting-entrepreneurship/women/wes-network/index_en.htm, referred 29/11/2013.

European Commission (2010): Gender pay statistics, http://epp.eurostat.ec.europa.eu/statistics_explained/index.php/Gender_pay_gap_st atistics, referred 29/11/2013.

European Commission (2010): Strategy for equality between women and men 2010 - 2015. Luxembourg: Publications Office of the European Union, http://ec.europa.eu/social/BlobServlet?docId=6568&langId=en, referred 29/11/2013.

European Commission (2008): Evaluation Policy: Promotion of Women Innovators and Entrepreneurship report. Brussels: European Commission, http://ec.europa.eu/enterprise/dg/files/evaluation/women_en.pdf, referred 28/11/2013.

European Foundation for the Improvement of Living and Working Conditions (2012): Employment trends and policies for older workers in the recession. Luxembourg: Publications Office of the European Union, http://www.eurofound.europa.eu/pubdocs/2012/35/en/1/EF1235EN.pdf, referred 29/11/2013.

European Foundation for the Improvement of Living and Working Conditions (2010): Family Life and Work - Second European Quality of Life Survey Family life and work report. Luxembourg: Publications Office of the European Union, http://www.eurofound.europa.eu/pubdocs/2010/02/en/1/EF1002EN.pdf, referred 29/11/2013.

European Institute for Gender Equity (2013): A study of collected narratives on gender perceptions in the 27 EU Member States Synthesis report, http://eige.europa.eu/sites/default/files/EIGE-study-on-collected-narratives-on-gender-perceptions-MH3112337ENC.pdf, referred 28/11/2013.

European Job Mobility Laboratory (2011): The Impact of the Crises on Senior Workers: Challenges and Responses by PES, http://www.mobilitypartnership.eu/Documents/EJML%20Senior%20workers%20final.pdf, referred 29/11/2013.

Eurostat (Statistical Office of the European Commission) (2012): online database, http://epp.eurostat.ec.europa.eu/portal/page/portal/statistics/themes, viewed 01/06/2012.

Eurostat (Statistical Office of the European Commission) (2012): online database, http://epp.eurostat.ec.europa.eu/portal/page/portal/statistics/themes, viewed 01/06/2012.

Eurostat (2012a): European Commission Eurostat: Your key to European statistics, http://epp.eurostat.ec.europa.eu/portal/page/portal/statistics/search_database, 05/09/2012.

Eurostat (Statistical Office of the European Commission) (2008): The life of women and men in Europe - a statistical portrait. Luxembourg: Publication Office of the European Union, http://epp.eurostat.ec.europa.eu/cache/ITY_OFFPUB/KS-80-07-135/EN/KS-80-07-135-EN.PDF, referred 29/11/2013.

Frevel, Alexander; Newiger-Bogumil, Carola (2012): Creative Management Strategies for SMEs in the Baltic Sea Region. Hamburg.

Geißler, H.; Bökenheide, T; Schlünkes, H.; Geißler-Gruber, B. (2007): Faktor Anerkennung. Betriebliche Erfahrungen mit wertschätzenden Dialogen. Frankfurt/New York.

Gdansk University of Technology:
http://www.themanagementor.com/kuniverse/kmailers_universe/manu_kmailers/bp_ensurecomp3.htm

Grzesiak, Marzena; Richter-Kaźmierska, Anita (15.07.2013): The analysis of the best practices' transfer, report produced within Work Package 3 of the EU-funded project BSR QUICK IGA, Gdansk, Poland.

Grzesiak, Marzena.; Olczyk, Magdalena; Starnawska, Marzena (30.06.2013): The best practices' transfer part I, report produced within Work Package 4 of the EU-funded project BRS QUICK-IGA, Gdansk, Poland.

Gruber, Brigitta / Frevel, Alexander / Vogel, Kaspar: Work Ability Coaching – a new tool encouraging individuals, businesses and industries to handle the demographic change process, in: Clas-Håkan Nygård/Minna Savinainen/Tapio Kirsi/Kirsi Lumme-Sandt (eds.) (2011): Age Management during the Life Course. Proceedings of the 4th Symposium on Work Ability. Tampere.

Gruber, Brigitta; Frevel, Alexander (2010): Wertschätzende Dialoge im Betrieb. Führung als Co-Produzent von Wohlbefinden, in: ergomed – Zeitschrift für arbeitsmedizinische Praxis und betriebliches Gesundheitsmanagement: 34. Jg., H. 1, S. 12-20.

Hasselhorn, Hans Martin; Freude, Gabriele (2007): Der Work Ability Index – ein Leitfaden. Schriftenreihe der Bundesanstalt für Arbeitsschutz und Arbeitsmedizin, Sonderschrift S 87. Dortmund / Berlin / Dresden.

Ilmarinen, Juhani (2007): The Work Ability Index (WAI), in: Occupational Medicine 2007; 57:160

Ilmarinen, Juhani (2005): Towards a Longer Worklife! Ageing and the quality of worklife in the European Union, Finnish Institute of Occupational Health / Ministry of Social Affairs and Health. Helsinki .

International Training Centre (2008): Break gender stereotypes, give talent a chance report. European Communities, http://www.businessandgender.eu/splash, referred 29/11/2013.

INQA – Initiative Neue Qualität der Arbeit: Arbeitsbewältigungs-Coaching - Der Leitfaden zur Anwendung im Betrieb [Text: Brigitta Gruber, Alexander Frevel] (2012). INQA-Bericht 38, Berlin (2. überarb. Aufl.).

Jones, M.K.; Latreille, P.L.; Sloane, P.J.; Staneva, A.V. (2011): Work-Related Health in Europe: Are Older Workers More at Risk report. Germany: Forschungsinstitut zur Zukunft der Arbeit - Institute for the Study of Labor, http://ftp.iza.org/dp6044.pdf, referred 29/11/2013.

Kaczmarek, B.; Sikorski, Cz.; Podstawy zarządzania (1998): Zachowania organizacyjne, Absolwent, Łódź, p. 24.

Kühntopf, Stephan; Tivig, Thusnelda (2009): Demographic Risk Atlas. Facts Behind the Maps, Schriftenreihe zur Nachhaltigkeit und CSR. Band 3. Rostock.

Nash, J.; Ehrenfeld, J. (1997): Codes of environmental management practice: assessing their potential as a tool for change. Annual Review of Energy and the Environment 22.

Nygård C-H.; Savinainen M.; Tapio K.; Lumme-Sandt K. (eds.) (2011): Age Management during the Life Course. Proceedings of the 4th Symposium on Work Ability. Tampere.

Piacentini, M. (2013): Women Entrepreneurs in the OECD: Key Evidence and Policy Challenges. OECD Social, Employment and Migration Working Papers, No. 147, OECD Publishing, http://dx.doi.org/10.1787/5k43bvtkmb8v-en, referred 28/11/2013.

Reed, P.; Kaplan, M.; Bowser, G. (2009): The Assistive Technology Trainer's Handbook. Roseburg: The NATE Network, http://www.natenetwork.org/manuals-forms/at-trainers-handbook, referred 29/11/2013.

Singh, Y.P. (1999): Training of Trainers manual. Haryana Forest Department, http://hcfp.gov.in/downloads/manuals/Training_of_Trainers_Manual.pdf, referred 22/05/2013.

Stabryła, A.; Trzcieniecki, J.; Organizacja i zarządzanie (1986): Zarys problematyki, Akademia Ekonomiczna w Krakowie, Kraków, p. 183–184.

Stiller, Silvia; Wedemeier, Jan (2011) (b): Wirtschaftsraum Ostsee: Städte auf Wachstumskurs, Wirtschaftsdienst 91 (8). Hamburg.

Tempel, Jürgen / Ilmarinen, Juhani (2013): Arbeitsleben 2025. Das Haus der Arbeitsfähigkeit im Unternehmen bauen. Hrsg. von Marianne Giesert, Hamburg.

The European Commission Mutual Learning Programme for Public Employment Services (2012): PES and older workers. European Commission, http://ec.europa.eu/social/keyDocuments.jsp?policyArea=&type=0&country=0&year=0&advSearchKey=PES+and+older+workers+2012&mode=advancedSubmit&langId=en, referred 29/11/2013.

Tikkanen, T.; Nuhan, B. (2006): Promoting lifelong learning for older workers report. Luxembourg: Publications Office of the European Union, http://www.cedefop.europa.eu/EN/Files/3045_en.pdf, referred 20.11.2013.

Tuomi, Kaija; Ilmarinen, Juhani; Jahkola, Antti; Katajarinne, Lea; Tulkki, Arto (1982): Work Ability Index. Finnish Institute of Occupational Health. Helsinki. [in german:] Hasselhorn, Hans Martin & Freude, Gabriele (2007): Der Work Ability Index – ein Leitfaden. Schriftenreihe der Bundesanstalt für Arbeitsschutz und Arbeitsmedizin, Sonderschrift S 87. Dortmund / Berlin / Dresden.

UNECE (2010): The unadjusted pay gap in the European Union report. Geneva: UNECE, http://epp.eurostat.ec.europa.eu/statistics_explained/index.php/Gender_pay_gap_st atistics, referred 29/11/2013.

Walker, A (2004): The emergence of age management in Europe. International Journal of Organizational Behavior, http://www.usq.edu.au/extrafiles/business/journals/HRMJournal/InternationalArti cles/Volume10Ageing/WalkerVol10-1.pdf, referred 29/11/2013.

Wallin, Marjo; Hussi, Tomi (2011): Best Practices in Age Management – Evaluation of Organisation Cases. FiOH. Helsinki.

Website of Abloy (2013): http://www.abloy.com/en/abloy/abloycom/About-ABLOY/Environmental-Responsibility/Age-Masters/, referred 29/11/2013.

Website of the Age Platform Europe (2013): http://www.age-platform.eu/index.php, referred 28/11/2013

Website of Business and Gender (2013): http://www.businessandgender.eu/en/home, referred 29/11/2013.

Website of Business and Professional Women (2013): http://www.bpw-europe.org/, referred 29/11/2013.

Website of Business Dictionary (2013): http://www.businessdictionary.com/definition/worst-case-scenario.html, referred 29/11/2013.

Website of EIGE (European Institute for Gender Equality) (2013): http://eige.europa.eu/, referred 29/11/2013.

Website of European Agency for Safety and Health at Work, Ageing Workers (2013): https://osha.europa.eu/en/priority_groups/ageingworkers/index_html, referred 29/11/2013.

Website of European Commission best practices (2012):
http://ec.europa.eu/dgs/secretariat_general/admin_burden/best_practice_report/best_practice_report_en.htm, referred 29/11/2013.

Website of European Employment Observatory (2013):
http://www.eu-employment-observatory.net/, referred 29/11/2013.

Website of European Small Business Portal (2013):
http://ec.europa.eu/small-business/index_en.htm, referred 29/11/2013.

Website of Eurostat (2013):
http://epp.eurostat.ec.europa.eu/portal/page/portal/statistics/themes, referred 29/11/2013.

Website of Micromentor (2013):
http://www.micromentor.org/resources/resource-center, referred 28/11/2013.

Website of Pan European Older Peoples Learning and Employment Network (2013):
http://www.europeanpeoplenetwork.eu/, referred 28/11/2013.

Website of SLIC, Sustainable Learning In the Community (2013):
http://www.slic-project.eu/trainingpf/slic2toolkit/index.php, referred 29/11/2013.

Website of YouTube (2013): Break gender stereotypes.
http://www.youtube.com/watch?feature=player_embedded&v=Qv8eWge8cu0, referred 29/11/2013.

Website of YouTube (2013): Women entrepreneurs could be answer to crisis.
http://www.youtube.com/watch?v=DQBVDYFwiGY&list=UUvhco_i3akl_yhKLgsjEcNA&index=4&feature=plcp, referred 29/11/2013.

Website of YouTube (2013): Carola Fischbach – Pyttel.
http://www.youtube.com/watch?feature=player_embedded&v=LQURPrp7xZQ, referred 29/11/2013.

Zwart B.; Frings-Dresen M. (2002): Test-retest reliability of the Work Ability Index questionnaire. Occupational Medicine; 52: 177–181.

Publications of the Baltic Sea Academy

Volume 1
Strategies for the Development of Crafts and SMEs
in the Baltic Sea Region
2011
ISBN: 9783842326125

Volume 2
Strategy Programme for education policies in the Baltic Sea Region
2012 (2nd edition)
ISBN: 9783848252534

Volume 3
Education Policy Strategies today and tomorrow around the "Mare Balticum"
2011
IBSN: 9783842374218

Volume 4
Energy Efficiency and Climate Protection around the
Mare Balticum
2011
ISBN: 9783844800982

Volume 5
SME relevant sectors in the BSR: Personnel organisation, Energy and
Construction
2012
ISBN: 9783848202577

Volume 6
Strategies and Promotion of Innovation in Regional Policies around the Mare
Balticum
2012
IBSN 9783848218295

Volume 7

Strategy Programme for innovation in regional policies in the Baltic Sea Region
2012
ISBN: 9783848230471

Volume 8

Humanivity - Innovative economic development through human growth by Kenneth Daun
2012
ISBN: 9783848253395

Volume 9

Economic Perspectives, Qualification and Labour Market Integration of Women in the Baltic Sea Region
2013
ISBN: 9783732243952

Volume 10

Corporate Social Responsebility and Women's Entrepreneurship around the Mare Balticum
2013
ISBN: 9783732278459

Volume 11

Development of the enterprises' competitiveness in the context of demographic challenges
2013
ISBN: 973732293971

Volume 12

Age, Gender and Innovation –

Strategy program and action plans for the Baltic Sea Region
2014
ISBN: 9783735784919

Volume 13

Innovative SMEs by Gender and Age around the Mare Balticum
2014
ISBN: 9783735791191

Volume 14

Innovation in SMEs, previous projects in the Baltic Sea Region and future needs
2014
ISBN: 9783735791191

Volume 15

Building the socially responsible employment policy in the Baltic Sea Region
2014
ISBN: 9783735790484

Volume 16

Women and elderly on the BSR labour market - good practices' analysis and transfer
2014
ISBN: 9783735791412

Volume 17

Manual and Best Practices for Innovative SMEs by Gender and Age in the Baltic Sea Region
2014
ISBN: 9783735791405

Members of the Hanse-Parlament

The Chamber of Craftmanship and Enterprise in Białystok

Brest Department of the Belarusian Chamber of Commerce and Industry

Hungarian Association of Craftsmen Corporations

Företagarna Kalmar länCottbus Chamber of Skilled Crafts and SME's

Dresden Chamber of Skilled Crafts and Small Businesses

Pomeranian Chamber of Handicrafts for SME's

Hamburg Chamber of Skilled Crafts and Small Businesses

The Federation of Finnish Enterprises

Chamber of Craft Region Kaliningrad

Kaliningrad Regional Economic Development Agency

Chamber of Crafts and SME in Katowice

Chamber of Crafts and SME in Kielce

Handicraft Chamber of Ukraine

Handicraft Chamber Leningrad Region

The Craft Chamber of Łódź

Företagarna Skåne Service AB

Belarusian Chamber of Commerce and Industry

Minsk Department of the Belarussian Chamber of Commerce and Industry

Mogilev Branch of Belarusian Chamber of Commerce and Industry

Russian Chamber of Crafts

Warmia and Mazury Chamber of Crafts and Small Business in Olsztyn

Chamber of Crafts in Opole

The Norwegian Federation of Craft Enterprises

Master of Crafts Norway

Eastern Mecklenburg-Western Pomerania Chamber of Handicraft

Panevėžys Chamber of Commerce, Industry and Crafts

Satakunnan Yrittajät R.Y.

Wielkopolska Craft Chamber in Poznań

Latvian Chamber of Crafts

Craft Chamber in Rzeszów

Schwerin Chamber of Skilled Crafts

The Chamber of Handicraft Middle Pomerania in Słupsk

The St. Petersburg Crafts Chamber

The Chamber of Crafts and SME in Szczecin

Estonian Association of Small and Medium Enterprises

The Baltic Institute of Finland

The Organisation of Handicraft Businesses in Trondheim

Vilnius Chamber of Commerce, Industry and Crafts

Lithuanian Business Employers Confederation

The Chamber of Crafts of Mazovia, Kurpie and Podlasie Regions in Warsaw

Small Business Chamber Warsaw

The Lower Silesian Chamber of Craft and Small and Medium-sized Businesses

Kyiv Chamber of Commerce and Industry

IBC Innovationsfabrikken Kolding

Donskaya Craft Chamber in Rostov/Don

Nordic Forum of Crafts

Members of the Baltic Sea Academy

Brest State Technical University, Belarus

University 21 non-profit limited Liability Company, Germany

Hamburg University of Corporate Education, Germany

Hamburg Institute of International Economics, Germany

Hanse-Parlament e.V., Germany

International Business Academy, Denmark

Lund University, Sweden

Satakunta University of Applied Sciences, Finland

University of Latvia, Latvia

Gdansk University of Technology, Poland

Panevėžys College

Hanseatic Academy of Management, Słupsk, Poland

Saint-Petersburg State University of Economics, Russia

Tampere University of Technology, Finland

Vilnius Gediminas Technical University, Lithuania

Vilnius Pedagogical University, Lithuania

University of Bialystok, Poland

Võru County Vacational Training Centre, Estonia